The
Rob Long
Omnibus Edition
of
Better Behaviour

The
Rob Long
Omnibus Edition
of
Better Behaviour

Rob Long

LONDON AND NEW YORK

First published 2005 by David Fulton Publishers in association with the National Association for Special Educational Needs (NASEN)

This collection first published 2007 by Routledge
2 Park Square, Milton Park, Abingdon OX14 4RN

Simultaneously published in the USA and Canada by Routledge
270 Madison Avenue, New York, NY 10016

Routledge is an imprint of the Taylor & Francis Group, an informa business

This collection is published in association with the National Association for Special Educational Needs (NASEN)

NASEN is a registered charity no. 1007023.

© 2005, 2007 Rob Long

Typeset by FiSH Books, Enfield, Middx.
Printed and bound in Great Britain by MPG Books Ltd, Bodmin

British Library Cataloguing in Publication Data
A catalogue record for this book is available from the British Library

Library of Congress Cataloging in Publication Data
A catalog record for this book has been applied for.

ISBN10 1-84312-470-X
ISBN13 978-1-84312-470-2

nasen is a professional membership association which supports all those who work with or care for children and young people with special and additional educational needs. Members include teachers, teaching assistants, support workers, other educationalists, students and parents.

nasen supports its members through policy documents, journals, its magazine *Special!*, publications, professional development courses, regional networks and newsletters. Its website contains more current information such as responses to government consultations. **nasen's** published documents are held in very high regard both in the UK and internationally.

Dedicated to the memory of Faraday John Davies
a valued friend and brother in arms

'To begin at the beginning'

Contents

Preface

This *Better Behaviour* omnibus edition brings together a series of books on behaviour written for busy school staff. The collection provides insight and understanding into a range of challenges and issues that are common in today's schools. It is of particular value in that it offers practical tips and strategies for dealing with each concern. More and more, school staff are expected to respond to an ever-increasing number of social, emotional, and behavioural difficulties that children and young people experience. The aim of any community school is to be inclusive. This naturally means that staff are now being challenged to create a learning environment that meets the needs of a small but significant group that has a range of diverse specific needs.

Chapter 1 **The Art of Positive Communication** emphasises the relationships between teachers and pupils, and between the pupils themselves. It explores how to build a good learning environment in which all pupils can achieve. This chapter includes sections on forming sound relationships, understanding non-verbal behaviour, accentuating the positive and eliminating the negative.

Chapter 2 **Better Behaviour** considers the difficulties faced by children that can so often become barriers to them learning. This chapter explains how teachers can help these pupils to face personal challenges and includes ideas for 'stress-proofing' children, guidance on teaching problem-solving skills, and an explanation and overview of cognitive behaviour therapy.

Chapter 3 **Children's Thoughts and Feelings** considers how a good understanding of how children think and feel can be the key to building good relationships in the classroom. This chapter contains information on underlying causes of emotional conflicts, the nature of maladaptive coping mechanisms, why boys tend to 'act out' and girls tend to 'act in', and interventions to promote the use of adaptive coping styles.

Chapter 4 focuses specifically on adolescent issues – **Yeah Right! Adolescents in the Classroom**. Is there more disruptive behaviour in schools today? The simple answer to this often asked question is probably 'Yes' – but the reasons lie more outside the teenagers than within. While we have all been teenagers, it was a unique time, and the issues are unique to any specific period – pressures differ, fears differ. Often schools unwittingly become part of the problem rather than part of the solution. Issues explored in this chapter are identity, autonomy, risk taking, and self-esteem.

Chapter 5 explores the ever difficult issue and concern of **Motivation**. Knowing how to interest and motivate pupils is a skill that separates the 'great' teachers from the mediocre. This chapter aims to inform and inspire staff and give them confidence in dealing with pupils who are not naturally 'teacher pleasers'. It includes sections on how personality affects learning styles, assessment tools and interventions, and how to reach the hard to teach.

Chapter 6 deals with an issue that all children experience in some form at some time in their development. **Loss and Separation** can be a very difficult subject for adults to manage. A sense of loss can have a very disturbing effect on children and can occur, not only as a result of bereavement, but also after divorce or separation, moving away from friends, moving between foster homes, for example. This chapter covers understanding loss, how different children react to loss, and listening to troubled children.

Chapter 7 looks at **Obsessive Compulsive Disorders**. Schools are often faced with supporting children who have mild forms of obsessive compulsive disorder. This chapter considers what obsessive compulsive disorders are, the causes, and how school staff can help the sufferer.

Finally, a key teaching skill is that of working with groups of children and young people, and Chapter 8 – **Working with Groups** – considers this area. Some learners will have emotional and behavioural difficulties. They may behave well in a one-to-one situation with an adult, but when they are in a group with their peers their behaviour deteriorates dramatically. The more staff understand of group dynamics, the better equipped they will be to support children who find such situations difficult. This chapter includes information on group skills, managing difficult groups, and the role of the group leader.

HOT TIP

On some pages in this chapter you will see a Hot Tip box containing quick-to-use positive communication techniques. So rather than waiting until you have read the whole chapter you can add to your existing communication skills as you go along.

 **The Art of Positive Communication**

Introduction

What is 'communication'?

This is a simple question about a process that we use all the time and yet is rarely considered. In every school, in every classroom, it is communication that sets the tone of any interaction between an adult and a young person. The interaction can be warm, friendly and enjoyable or it may be soured with negativity and hostility. A well-turned phrase can make or break a student's day.

Communication is the process by which information ('the message') is sent from one person – the sender – to another – the receiver. Messages are made up of many components:

verbal
- words

nonverbal
- tone of voice
- facial expressions
- body stance
- gestures
- proximity.

It is through listening to the whole message, by paying attention to the nonverbal cues, that we are able to understand not only what is said but also the emotional state of the person. The way that we say 'It's good to see you', for example, carries more information than the words themselves. The tone of the speaker's voice, degree of eye contact and body posture will each affect the way in which the message is interpreted regarding the emotional state of the speaker. Listening is an active process but, because it takes place so quickly and subconsciously, we are – for most of the time – unaware of it.

We may speak with our voices but we communicate with our whole body. Everything that a sender says or does can be interpreted as part of the message, and up to 90% of the message is sent nonverbally.

The number of communications we make each day is phenomenal and, because they are so frequent and so natural, we rarely take the time to reflect on our particular style. This book will enable you to review key aspects of your own communication style as well as to consider some different techniques for handling those 'difficult situations' that all school staff meet during the day. These include the times when students carry on talking while class instructions are being given, demand excessive attention or use inappropriate language.

Our students have a sense of how we feel about them from the way we talk to them. Young people are influenced by the way in which adults relate to them and positive relationships develop from positive communication skills. Schools encourage and support students in many ways – through the use of rewards and certificates, for example – but one of the most powerful, and sometimes least understood, forms of encouragement, is in the feedback adults give to students, which can affect their self-esteem.

Self-assessment

Before we go any further it might be helpful to take a snapshot of how you feel about your existing communication skills by completing the questionnaire on the following pages.

Do you communicate positively?

Circle Y (yes), N (no) or S (sometimes) in response to the following statements:

- I always listen to my students' points of view.   Y   N   S
- I smile and laugh with my students.   Y   N   S
- I ask misbehaving students what helped them last time the
  situation occurred.   Y   N   S
- My behaviour management approach is to 'catch them doing good'.   Y   N   S
- I often leave a student with a choice and then withdraw.   Y   N   S
- When giving instructions I say 'thank you' rather than 'please'.   Y   N   S
- Initially I use the lightest intervention possible to correct behaviour. Y   N   S
- When correcting behaviour I avoid being distracted. I stay focused. Y   N   S

- If students are angry I raise my voice, but do not get angry myself.   Y   N   S
- If a student is being disruptive I ask him/her to say which class rule is being broken.   Y   N   S
- I criticise the behaviour that prevents the task at hand, not the person.   Y   N   S
- I encourage students to recognise and value their efforts and progress.   Y   N   S
- I make a point of hearing the students' issues when problems occur.   Y   N   S
- When possible I help students understand the emotions they are feeling and why.   Y   N   S
- I remind misbehaving students of the consequences of their behaviour.   Y   N   S
- To improve behaviour I ask students what it is that they should be doing.   Y   N   S
- I make sure students know that I am looking out for improvements.   Y   N   S
- I assure students that working together we can find a better way forward.   Y   N   S
- I often remind students of previous agreements, such as to ask for help from the teaching assistant.   Y   N   S
- I use a wide and varied range of positive verbal descriptions of behaviour, such as 'clever', 'imaginative', 'interesting', 'creative', etc.   Y   N   S

Your score
Yes _____   No _____   Sometimes _____

Interpretation of your score

Note that different questions in the above list focus on different communication skills, which you should be aware of when checking your score:

- language and listening skills: nos. 1, 2, 6, 12, 14, 20
- solution-focused responses: nos. 3, 4, 10, 16, 17, 19
- reactions to misbehaviour: nos. 5, 7, 8, 9, 11, 13, 15, 18.

How many questions did you answer with a positive 'Yes'?

Above 15
You are already a skilled communicator.

Between 10 and 15
You are competent and aware of areas to develop.

Below 10
This book is the start of developing your communication skills.

HOT TIP

Here and now

To enhance a positive sense of community use 'we' and 'our' rather than 'I' and 'my'. For example you might observe: 'This is one of the class rules that we all discussed and agreed on last week: that we would listen to other people's viewpoints without interrupting them.' Similarly a teacher might say, 'One of our golden rules is that we always put our hand up to answer questions.' Use students' names often. Give immediate nonverbal feedback – smiling, positive gestures, eye contact.

Whatever your score, being an effective communicator is a key skill that will benefit from having an 'MOT'. The fact is that we have each developed our own communication style that has been influenced by a range of factors such as:

- family experiences – how our parents praised and corrected our own behaviour
- temperament – some of us are naturally more volatile and easier to anger than others
- educational background – how we learnt to reflect about our own behaviour.

We each have a preferred way of relating to students in difficult and challenging situations. When students express needs that interfere either with others' learning, our teaching, or both, we react automatically according to our mental template.

Can you detect your communication style?

Without pausing to reflect, read the statements below and quickly confirm Yes or No.

Do you AVOID and try to withdraw?

- There are times when I let others take responsibility for solving the problem.   Y   N
- I try to do whatever it takes to avoid unnecessary tensions.   Y   N
- I sometimes avoid taking positions which would create controversy.   Y   N
- If it makes other people happy, I might let them maintain their views.   Y   N
- I feel that differences are not always worth worrying about.   Y   N
- I'd rather concede a point than have an argument.   Y   N

Do you ACCOMMODATE and try to smooth out differences?

- Rather than negotiate the things on which we disagree, I try to stress those things upon which we both agree.   Y   N
- I might try to soothe the other person's feelings and preserve our relationship.   Y   N
- I sometimes sacrifice my own wishes for the wishes of the other person.   Y   N
- I try not to hurt the other person's feelings.   Y   N
- If it makes other people happy, I might let them maintain their views.   Y   N
- In approaching negotiations, I try to be considerate of the other person's wishes.   Y   N

Do you COMPETE and try to win at all costs?

- I will never give in without a fight.   Y   N
- I try to win my position.   Y   N
- I am usually firm in pursuing my goals.   Y   N
- I make some effort to get my way.   Y   N
- I press to get my points made.   Y   N
- I assert my wishes.   Y   N

Do you COLLABORATE and try to problem-solve?

- I attempt to deal with all of the other person's concerns and my own.   Y   N
- I consistently seek the other person's help in working out a solution.   Y   N
- I always share the problem with the other person so that we can work it out.   Y   N

- I attempt immediately to work through our differences.   Y   N
- I always lean toward a direct discussion of the problem.   Y   N
- In approaching negotiations I try to be considerate of the other
  person's wishes.   Y   N

Do you COMPROMISE and ensure that there is a 'win–win' outcome?

- I try to find a compromise solution.   Y   N
- I give up some points in exchange for others.   Y   N
- I will let the other person have some of his/her positions if s/he lets
  me have some of mine.   Y   N
- I try to find a fair combination of gains and losses for both of us.   Y   N
- I propose a middle ground.   Y   N
- I am nearly always concerned with satisfying all our wishes.   Y   N

Interpretation of your answers

Place your yes score in the radar graph below to discover your communication style. No style is in itself right or wrong – the problem arises when we over-use one style irrespective of the circumstances. High 'yes' scores in any style may reflect an over-reliance on that style. The ability to be flexible is a strength. You may well find that you have an even profile – which is normal. Specific troughs highlight areas to develop.

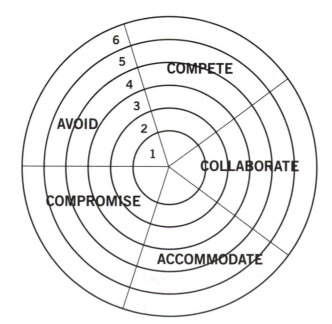

FIGURE 1.1 Radar graph

Forming relationships: accentuate the positive

It is strange that the one subject that we all experience and value is the one thing we receive the least training in: relationships. It is relationships that give our lives meaning yet they are the one thing that we receive little help with – until they go wrong.

We each experience relationships through our own frame of reference, which is part of our cultural identity. We select, organise and interpret our world through the influence of our culture and, without being directly conscious of it, our values and beliefs shape the meaning we find in any relationship. It is important to appreciate that it is for this reason that no two people experience any interaction in exactly the same way. It also follows that, if our values and beliefs differ greatly from another person's, then it can prevent us from understanding their method of communication. This explains why we find some students easier to relate to than others. As professionals we need to be aware of and actively explore the cultural frame of reference through which our students view the learning context.

Listening

True communication involves listening as well as talking. (It is interesting that we have two ears and only one mouth.) Too often we concentrate on the sending side of the communication equation, not the listening side, because most of us think we are naturally good listeners. Real listening is called 'active listening' and, when working with young people, it is as fundamental as sending the message. Listening enhances rapport in a relationship because it shows that you are concerned and wish to understand what is being said.

HOT TIP

Paradoxical instruction

If a difficult and defiant student decides to walk away from you say to them, 'That's OK. You go for a walk and we will talk about this later.' The student is now not defying you but instead carrying out your instructions and not being defiant.

7

Three main barriers to listening

Response rehearsal

We are too busy rehearsing in our head what we are going to say when the other person stops speaking because, for example, we want to tell them something interesting that happened to us yesterday.

Preoccupied

When we have personal worries these can drain our energy and stop us from concentrating on what is being said. We find that our mind keeps returning to our own concern (such as our overdraft) rather than truly listening to the other person.

Stimulus reactions

Certain words or phrases can have such strong emotional associations for us that when we hear them we are immediately distracted from hearing the message being sent. For example, someone says the word 'audit' and we are reminded that in four weeks' time Ofsted are coming and we are not ready.

Active listening

Good listening involves attending to many messages at the same time and being able to select and respond to those most relevant. There is a lot of 'noise' in any communication – that is, irrelevant and distracting information. As a result we do not always correctly receive and interpret the message that is being sent. 'You told me that you were really happy in school. But the way you said it, the tone of your voice and your body posture, made me think that you were anything but happy.'

The main difference between everyday listening and active listening is that in active listening the listener makes every effort to check that he or she really understands what is being said as well as helping the speaker understand it him/herself. Before moving on to consider how we send messages we need to highlight some of the key skills of effective listening. Some you will recognise as already being part of your repertoire; others might be new and need practising.

Key skills of effective listening

Encouraging

The right sort of encouragement enables a student to feel safe enough to make a contribution. Young people are often more used to being told what they should

> **HOT TIP**
>
> **Secondary behaviours**
>
> Students can be very clever at distracting adults from their focus. Secondary behaviours such as looking away, the sneer, and the mumbled comment can all result in the adult switching his/her attention from the target concern to another concern – which is of the student's making. Stay focused: 'We need to talk about your lack of homework. If we can't do so now I will see you later.'

think or do, or being questioned about their behaviour. Open-ended questions can lend support to the feeling that the listener genuinely wants to hear their views. Examples might be:

- 'You are doing a really good job. What are you planning to do next?'
- 'Look how much better you are getting on now. What skills have you used to achieve this?'

Paraphrasing
By paraphrasing what the student has said you show understanding of the message that he or she has 'sent'. For example you might say:

- 'Let's see if I've got this right. You're saying that you are less anxious during playtimes than you were last week?'
- 'So what we have talked about so far is this. You have changed your route home and always wait for your two friends.'

Summarising
By summarising what the young person has said you show understanding of the main points contained within several messages, for example:

- 'To sum it up, then. What you are saying is that when you sit at the front of the class you can hear other children calling you names and it is making you very tense and frightened. Would you agree with that?'

Clarifying
This is necessary to establish meaning when the message is confused or uncertain, such as:

- 'What do you mean when you say you feel put upon?'
- 'Can I just see if I have got this right? When the instructions are written down for you, you don't have to worry about remembering them?'
- 'I am not sure if I understand you. Could you tell me a bit more? If I was in the playground with you, what would I see happening?'

Empathising

Empathising with the young person shows them your appreciation of their feelings. You might say:

- 'I understand how having someone push in front of you made you feel very angry.'
- 'I know you are feeling sad that your best friend is moving away.'
- 'With all the work you have to do to catch up it's not surprising that you feel worried.'

Probing

Sometimes it is necessary to probe in order to obtain more information about a subject that the young person has introduced but not fully explained. You might ask, for example:

- 'Can you tell me more about what Sam was doing to stop you working?'
- 'Can you think of an example of the games that you feel unhappy about joining in with?'

Challenging

You may need to challenge young people when their ideas or actions seem to conflict, for example:

- 'Isn't this different from what you were just telling me? You said one of your best friends was Joanna.'

HOT TIP

Visual displays

Display your Class Rules visually. When a rule is broken, point to the relevant part and just say 'Rule 3'.

- 'I'm confused. On the one hand you seem to be saying that you enjoy your time out of class for extra help, but now you're telling me that you are being made to feel different from the rest of the class.'

Linking

This helps the student to reflect on ideas that appear to relate, such as:

- 'Earlier you said you really enjoyed PE – football especially – and now you're saying you wish you had some out-of-school interests.'
- 'Can you see any similarities between what you are saying now about how much you enjoy listening to music and what you said earlier about being unsure of which subjects to take next year?'

Descriptive observation

This helps the young person to find possible meanings in what they have said or done. This might be by saying, for example:

- 'You said you were happy that you had a change of teacher, but you sounded so sad.'
- 'Do you notice that whenever you mention William, you smile?'

When you start to listen actively don't be surprised that you keep making such mistakes as:

- interrupting
- asking too many questions
- offering solutions.

Whenever we try to break old habits relapse is normal. The more you practise, however, the quicker you will establish new habits.

HOT TIP

Ask good questions

Asking 'why?' questions usually leads to a defensive response. Instead ask 'what?' or 'how?' A good question is, 'What would you like to have happen?' It encourages the student to focus on a positive goal.

Nonverbal behaviour

It is so easy in a learning context to take an over-rational view of both ourselves and our students. We forget – at our peril – the fact that we each have cultural and biological templates through which all information is perceived. These lead us to obtain much more information, albeit subconsciously, from nonverbal cues than from verbal ones. Our brain, for example, is pre-programmed with 'fight or flight' responses to danger. As a result a finger being waved in our face might cause a stronger reaction than might be expected. Similarly, as a culture we tend to stand at a certain, acceptable distance from each other. If someone enters our 'personal space' we can feel threatened.

When you ask a friend, 'How are you?' and they reply, 'I'm fine', you might respond, 'What's wrong?' because you have detected in their intonation a clear sign of unhappiness. This confirms the adage, 'It ain't what you say, it's the way that you say it.'

Following from this, within the classroom the way we convey information nonverbally can have a huge impact on our relationship with our students. Below is a list of those areas to be aware of, as well as ideas as to how we can convey our respect and value for our students without even thinking about the content of what we are saying.

The term 'nonverbal behaviour' covers:

- facial expressions
- voice intonation
- gestures and postures.

Through nonverbal behaviours we can convey:

- interest vs. boredom
- affection vs. hostility
- concern vs. disregard.

HOT TIP

Selective listening

Remember, many students will be looking for your buttons – those things that you overreact to. Practise ignoring minor behaviour disturbances – stay with the positive.

HOT TIP

The power of silence

After you give an instruction to a student take two deep breaths and pause while you wait for compliance. Say no more than is absolutely necessary.

As emotional beings, it is what is not said that conveys the messages we most wish to hear. Do you like me? Are you interested in me? Will you help me if I get stuck?

Nonverbal behaviour can be either positive or negative:

Positive nonverbal behaviours
- smiling
- eye contact
- meeting and greeting
- thanking
- avoiding intensive eye contact
- having your hands visual and open
- not entering students' personal space
- avoiding finger pointing
- showing concern
- not being over-calm.

Negative nonverbal behaviours
- pointing can be interpreted as threat
- talking to the board shows more interest in the content than in the students
- invading a student's personal space with intense eye contact can trigger negative reactions
- shouting – your normal voice shows you are in control – the louder the voice the more the message is one of 'losing control'
- folding arms conveys a stand-offish attitude.

De-escalating conflict through nonverbal behaviours

When we are trying to impress or develop a friendship we subconsciously reflect the behaviour of the person we are interacting with. This is known as 'mirroring'.

13

What is going on is a conversation between two people at a subconscious level. We take up a not dissimilar body posture and we modify how close we stand to each other so that we both feel comfortable. We develop an appropriate amount of eye contact and we 'take turns' in our conversations. A relationship develops through each of us subtly influencing the other's behaviours. When these processes do not take place normal relationships do not flourish.

Within a working relationship there is, then, a sense of reciprocity: 'You can influence me and I can influence you.'

HOT TIP

Put the behaviour on the chair

When you challenge their behaviour students can easily believe that you don't like them. We understand the 'condemn the act not the child' motto, but it is not that easy for a young person. Write the behaviours that you are concerned about on a list and place the list on a chair. Explain to the student that it is these behaviours that you have a problem with, not them. You wish to work with them to improve these behaviours.

The reason young people so often have major confrontations with adults they do not know is that there is no history between them of one affecting the other's behaviour. Without that they can both become locked into an escalating spiral of confrontation – with neither being able to reduce the conflict. This is why *all* students are more positively manageable when we have established a relationship with them. As professionals, the more we can understand the nature of these 'off-stage' subconscious and nonverbal conversations the more we can constructively use them. We can ensure that the messages we are sending out are the ones we wish our students to receive, for example that we are firm and confident rather than aggressive and threatening.

When a student is agitated and becoming angry we can use nonverbal signals to help return them to a more normal state. Simply telling them to calm down can add fuel to an already inflamed situation, and any level of arousal in our own voice shows the student that his/her emotional state has affected ours. We need to modify our own behaviour to send out calming messages in an attempt to reduce the student's level of arousal, with calmer hand gestures, less threatening body language and non-confrontational words. Our knowledge of body language gives us a set of skills to manage individuals and groups of students. Without this it would be as though we were driving in a foreign country without a road map.

> **HOT TIP**
>
> **Small problems need small tools**
>
> Use the lightest touch to manage behaviour – avoid overreacting. There is no need to 'use a sledgehammer to crack a nut'.

An old teachers' saying about students goes: 'They don't care how much you know until they know how much you care.' As you convey your respect and care for students you are investing in the emotional bank. If at a later time you need students to comply with a request they are more likely to, and if you make mistakes they are more likely to forgive you. It is worth paying attention to the messages you are conveying with your nonverbal behaviour in order to deter unnecessary power struggles.

Eliminate the negative

Messages and feelings

We all have ways of communicating with our students that we have learned from our own past experiences. Some of these are less effective than others – in fact, they can make difficult matters worse.

What happens is that we can be saying one thing but our nonverbal messages can be contradicting the verbal content. The nonverbal part of the message – communicated through tone of voice, body posture, facial expressions, eye contact, proximity and use of silence, are interpreted subconsciously – and affect the way the total message is received.

In the classroom an adult can convey his/her sense of uncertainty through such behaviours as pacing, fidgeting, self-grooming, etc. All of these will correctly be seen by students as signs of insecurity. This contrasts with the adult who has a more relaxed but controlled posture – in-control teachers will often lean casually on furniture.

Some ineffective communication ploys

Some examples of negative ways of addressing students are given below. No doubt you can add to this list.

15

HOT TIP

Let's rewind

When a student says or does something inappropriate don't react immediately. Give them an opportunity to change it. Say, 'I don't think that worked as well as it could have. Let's rewind it and see if we can do it better.' This can save a lot of minor problems unnecessarily escalating.

Sarcasm

- 'You knew you had a test today but you still managed to leave your book at home. That was pretty smart! We await your results with interest.'

- 'Is this your homework? I will have to take up Chinese to be able to read it.'

Threats

- 'Touch that switch once more and you'll be in detention.'

- 'If you don't spit that gum out this minute, I'm going to send you out of my lesson.'

Commands

- 'Clean up this room right now. I will not take no for an answer.'

- 'Help me carry these boxes in. Hurry up!'

Prophecy

- 'You lied to me about your homework, didn't you? Do you know what kind of person you are going to be when you grow up? A person nobody can trust, and nobody will like.'

- 'Just keep going on being selfish. You'll see, no one is ever going to want to be friends with you. They'll treat you as badly as you're treating people now. Then we'll see how you like it.'

Lecturing and moralising

- 'Do you think that was a nice thing to do – to grab that book from your friend? I can see you don't realise how important good manners are. What you have to understand is that if we expect people to be polite to us, then we must be polite to them in return. You wouldn't want anyone to grab things from you, would you? Then you shouldn't grab from anyone else. We do unto others as we would have others do unto us.'

HOT TIP

The Columbo strategy

Like the TV detective Columbo, be prepared to ask for the student's assistance: 'I've never worked with a student like you before. You've had lots of people try to help you. What would you try if you were in my shoes?'

It is so easy to produce in students the very opposite feelings from those we intend to. When students are disciplined in such ways there are basically one of two responses open to them.

Fight vs. flight

These biologically programmed responses result in either offensive behaviour – 'acting out' – or defensive behaviour – 'acting in'. Neither is good for learning. The characteristics of each are as follows:

Acting out
- verbally abusive
- disruptive
- threatening and challenging
- defiant
- angry.

Acting in
- passive withdrawal
- lack of initiative
- dependency on others
- self-blame
- guilt.

Confrontational and challenging communications will typically increase both offensive and defensive behaviour. Instead, by the use of positive communication techniques students who demonstrate either of these categories of behaviour can be managed in a positive and non-confrontational way. Different techniques are presented here for managing the two types of behaviour, but are not exclusive to each.

Techniques for managing students who are acting out

- Make sure the student is alert and attending to you before you attempt to talk to him/her. Use the student's name and make brief eye contact.

- Ask positive questions, such as 'Can you remember what you did last time that helped sort out this argument about using the computer?' Make sure your questions are constructive; that is, 'What should you be doing?' rather than, 'What are you doing?'

- Indicate consequences. Point out the problem behaviour and the consequences of it. For example, 'If you persist with shouting out you will have to stay behind to discuss the rule about how to get attention in my class in detail.' Instead of whining, 'Why can't you line up nicely?' say, 'Until there is no pushing and pulling we will not be able to go in for dinner.'

- Offer choices, such as, 'You have two choices. You can either return to your maths work or you can have five minutes to finish off your art work. I will come back shortly to see which you have chosen.'

- Demonstrate positive expectations of students: 'Now please put all the equipment away so that we are ready to begin the next task,' or, 'You need to put a lot more effort into your work to achieve the grade you are capable of.' Instead of highlighting negative behaviour – 'You are still fooling around' – tell them what you are looking for – 'I expect you to be settled and working on your next target.'

- Make it short and snappy. If a student is not wearing their jacket, instead of a long explanation, just say 'jacket'. If they are eating inappropriately, 'bin'.

- Focus on behaviour. Make clear to students that it is their behaviour that is the problem, not them. Write the problem behaviour down and place it on a seat – this helps them to focus on the problem as something separate from themselves. Explain to the student that you want to work with them to help them to manage the behaviour better.

- Be solution-focused. Instead of analysing the problem help the student understand what the conditions are that enable them to behave appropriately. For example, instead of trying to understand the explanation as to why the student had a fight during lunchtime yesterday, try to help him/her explain why s/he did not get into a fight today. What was happening that prevented it? Who was the student with? What were they doing?

- Sensitively inject humour into the situation as a distracting technique. If a student is drawing cartoons instead of reading the set task, say, 'If we go on losing time like this I'll be retired before we find a solution to the science problem.'

HOT TIP

Something special

Find out what a student's special interest is. Then, for example, one day bring them a relevant magazine and say to them, 'I saw this in the market and couldn't help but think that you would be interested in it.'

- Side-step confrontations. Be prepared to withdraw from a confrontation. For example, when a student claims they have not had their work back, say, 'We need to have a chat about this at the end of the lesson.'

- Provide distractions. Prepare a range of activities such as an ongoing project, a physical task of sorting equipment out or a message that needs to be taken somewhere. You can divert a student's attention with this when they are finding a certain task challenging.

- Show faith: say 'when' not 'if'. 'When' shows a definite expectation that the student will succeed, whereas 'if' shows doubt. For example, 'When you have finished that piece of work you can have ten minutes on the computer,' rather than, 'You can go on the computer if you finish the work.'

- 'Follow instructions with a 'thank you' rather than a 'please'. 'Thank you' shows an assumption that your instructions will be carried out: 'Back in the queue, thank you.'

Techniques for managing students who are acting in

- Skill development. Find out about students' interests and support them in enhancing and strengthening their skills through providing safe opportunities. If they are interested in cooking, for example, this can be used as some part of a project.

- Build self-esteem. Students will often feel negative towards themselves through seeing others who are more able and confident. Develop a daily programme to help raise their self-esteem. This would include relaxation activities, target-setting for success, time with friends, humour through watching favourite TV programmes, good self-care habits (such as diet and exercise).

- Send a student a note highlighting a success or thanking them for their help in some area. Many students rarely receive unsolicited appreciation from adults.

- Thought-stopping: teach the student to change their thinking. Help them to re-establish some positive memories and encourage them to practise thinking of them when they are feeling negative. An elastic band on the wrist can be pulled to help them snap out of the negative. The sudden snap can trigger them to stop the negative thinking and do something different.

- Target-setting. Succeeding at challenging but achievable targets will help to encourage students' positive views of themselves – providing they accept that it is their effort, not luck, that produced the result.

- Personalise feedback. Use a special term or name; for example if I only ever say 'you are my top scientific wizard' to one pupil it will have more impact. If you call everybody 'a star' then being a star is not special.

- Worry time. When students face issues that cannot be readily resolved teach them to have a short worry period – five minutes – after which they must get back on task. If the worrying thoughts try to creep in before the allotted time they must tell them to wait.

- Positive thinking. Spend time with students to help them appreciate the skills they have mastered over the years. Reinforce the notion that it was practice and determination that led to their success. Also encourage them to see many of their personal qualities as attributes that others like in them. Often what we see in ourselves as a vice our friends can see as a positive and enduring virtue.

- Story-telling. To help a student confront unpleasant situations and fears find relevant stories that explore similar issues in a positive way. For a student who is being bullied, for example, a story or TV soap that deals sensitively with this topic could be a useful learning and talking point. We all find it easier to confront our fears one remove from ourselves – the emotional arousal is less, enabling us to consider the strategies that are used in the story.

- Relaxation. Exercises to relax muscles through tensing then relaxing, combined with breathing techniques (breathe in through the nose to the count of seven and out through the mouth to the count of ten), will help those students who are prone to anxiety. Once these skills are taught students can practise them anywhere and at any time.

- Catch them being good, for example, 'I really liked your contribution in the history lesson yesterday.' Be solution-focused instead of always analysing the difficulties: 'What do you think helped you to work so well for the last half of my lesson?' Find the 'exceptions' to any problem, that is when the problem is not as bad as usual: 'I noticed that you left your seat less than you usually do. Why do you think that was?' When things have gone well, help the student understand those factors that enabled that to happen. Such knowledge can be used to make these exceptions happen more often.

- Assertiveness training. From an understanding of their rights, as well as the rights of others, students can learn how to express themselves, manage

HOT TIP

What's in it for me?

Before helping students develop an action plan, improve their determination to change by helping them see what is 'in it for them'.

confrontations and negotiate as well as how to accept criticism and receive compliments.

- Anchoring and mood-changing. A student can learn to trigger positive emotions through taking a strong, positive memory and exploring it in the fullest detail. Where are they? What are they wearing? Who are they with? What are the positive feelings they have inside? Now teach a basic behavioural cue – crossing two fingers. The student practises crossing fingers and re-experiencing the emotions associated with the memory. At times of negativity the trigger – crossing fingers – can pull out the positive feelings.

- Problem-solving. Negative feelings usually tell us that things are not right for us. Teach the students how to explore a problem, generate possible solutions, choose one of those solutions to tackle the problem with, and afterwards to evaluate outcome. If, for example, the student is shy help them to explore ways of relaxing. Talk to them about those situations that they can manage and help them practise taking control of their feelings. Problems can be reframed as opportunities to improve these essential skills.

Some of the ideas in the above two lists are clearly applicable both to students who 'act out' and those who 'act in'. Never let an imposed classification system stop you using common sense – go with whatever technique helps an individual student.

Conclusion

To conclude then, good communication skills are the strongest tool that school staff have. Our voices are always with us. The tips and techniques detailed in this chapter will be familiar to many staff, and will encourage new staff to look carefully at their communication style. Positive communication is an effective way to manage young people's behaviour: it minimises stress and is successful and enjoyable.

Recommended reading

Bocchino, R. (1999) *Emotional Literacy*. Thousand Oaks, California: Corwin Press.

Brophy, J. (1998) *Motivating students to learn*. Boston, Massachusetts: McGraw Hill.

Friend, M. and Cook, L. (2000) *Interactions*. New York: Addison Wesley Longman.

Neall, L. (2002) *Bringing the best out of boys*. Stroud: Hawthorn Press.

Partin, R. (1999) *Classroom Teacher's Survival Guide*. West Nyack, New York: The Centre for Applied Research in Education.

Mackenzie, R. (1996) *Setting Limits in the Classroom*. Roseville, California: Prima Publishing.

Weare, K. (2000) *Promoting Mental and Social Health*. London: Routledge.

2 | Better Behaviour

Introduction

Life is not, and will never be, problem free, no matter what one's circumstances are. Neither is it fair. However, all school staff will have worked with children who have had more than their fair share of problems. The need has never been greater for children to acquire the necessary skills to cope with the challenges they are going to face in everyday life. This chapter aims to give school staff practical ideas, based on sound theory and evidence, to support children who are experiencing problems.

We know that in school children face a wide range of challenges. These include:

- specific and general learning difficulties
- communication difficulties
- physical problems
- sensory disabilities
- medical problems
- emotional, social and behavioural difficulties
- loss and separation.

We also know that the high rate of family breakdown in the UK inevitably means that children either witness or are caught up in it. Harold, Pryor and Reynolds (2001) note that, in 1998, 55% of divorcing couples in England and Wales had one child or more under the age of 16. Of these children, 26% were under the age of five, and 45% were between the ages of five and ten. It is clear, then, that at times of significant development a large number of children are under considerable stress.

Furthermore, one child out of every four is admitted to hospital before the age of five in the UK. And over 800,000 children per year are hospitalised. Some 30% of these hospitalisations occur after an emergency admission due to some form of accident.

The number of children growing up in poverty also remains depressingly high. The Institute for Fiscal Studies (Emerson, 2001) reported that over 4 million children were living in poverty in 1995–6. This is three times the number reported to be in poverty twenty years before.

Better Behaviour takes the view that, while we have high expectations regarding behaviour, we do not always spend the time teaching children how to behave. While each child has an inner drive to achieve his or her potential, many children face barriers that get in the way of their healthy growth and development. Many symptoms in children that adults view as problems are, in fact, the manifestation of the children's efforts to overcome their difficulties and have their needs met.

The conflict stems from children falling back on half-developed strategies to deal with any challenges that face them. If they had better strategies for confronting challenges they would have fewer difficulties resulting from their misguided response to them.

Much of any school's time is spent in sorting out these difficulties. This is a reactive approach and will never get to the root of the problem, which is that many children lack the necessary skills to cope in the situations in which they find themselves.

It would be over-bold to claim that the answer lies within the pages of this book. Instead, its aims are more modest: namely, to support the efforts of those school staff who have an interest in the whole child and, more precisely, the inner child. How many of us have sat feeling helpless at some of the challenges that children face? The boy who is waiting for the operation to stretch both his legs in order to help overcome his restricted growth. Or the girl who has a hole in the heart and is coping with her own understanding as well as the fears that she sees in the eyes of others around her. Must we sit passively by, waiting for the event to come and go? *Better Behaviour* provides some ideas, in a user-friendly way, for the caring practitioner to explore and build upon.

Some years ago two men eminent in their own fields were discussing the research proposal of one of them, Martin Seligman. Seligman is a psychologist who has done considerable research into depression. He was arguing for money to enable him to set up a programme to develop positive thinking in children: he wanted to produce 'the optimistic child'. His colleague, Professor Salk, was the inventor of the polio vaccine which has saved countless children's lives as well as reducing the number who suffered paralysis. Salk agreed with Seligman's aims and explained to him that he was wishing to do what he, Salk, had also done, that is to 'psychologically immunise' children against the negative influences of their time. This chapter is a reflection of their ideas.

The suggestions that follow come from a wide range of theories to do with healthy child development. Techniques are presented that are the outcome of our increased understanding of 'resiliency', that is, how some children can remain healthy in unhealthy situations. Sometimes it is useful to study something that is working, rather than always studying something that has broken down. The approach that was used in the past explains why adolescence is seen by many as a time of 'storm and stress': the only adolescents studied were those who were experiencing adjustment difficulties – and nobody studied the vast majority of adolescents who did not develop these problems.

The effectiveness and validity of the ideas explored in this chapter will depend on the developmental stage of the child in question. It may be helpful for the practitioner to look at an overview of child development (see Figure 2.1). Figure 2.2 highlights and helps us to appreciate the 'normal' challenges faced by children at different age milestones.

Stress-proofing

A child's nervous system operates with a functional level of arousal: just like a car engine it needs to be switched on. When children are awake and aware of their surroundings they have the mental capacity to deal with the learning challenges that face them, such as engaging in play with peers and attending to school work. But if this arousal increases on account of other challenges, such as worries from home or anxiety about an operation, then the system moves from functional arousal into stress. To continue with the car analogy, the accelerator is now pumping more petrol into the system than is needed. When we know what to do in a situation we cope effectively, for example '2 + 3 = ?' is not a problem because we can easily retrieve the solution. Stress is either a) when pressures we could have coped with one at a time make simultaneous demands or b) when a single event overwhelms us. Stress, then, is a general term that describes the negative outcome of an individual's response to certain events within his or her world. These events can be real or imagined. How one child responds to losing a game might be with sulks and tears, while his or her friend becomes determined to learn to play better and a third throws the game on the floor aggressively.

DEV. \ AGE	CHILDHOOD		ADOLESCENCE	
	EARLY 3 to 6	MIDDLE 6 to 11	EARLY 11 to 15	MIDDLE 15 to 18
PHYSICAL	physical growth slow, gross motor skills – running, jumping mastered	bike riding mastered and improved fine motor skills early signs of puberty	rapid changes secondary sex characteristics less motor control – clumsy	growth slows down boys catch up with girls
EMOTIONAL	limited emotional vocabulary – emotions shown through behaviour	more complex emotions – pride, guilt and shame more sensitive and empathic	anxious, self-conscious and angry sexual feelings strong moody	less defensive and more able to express their emotions anxiety about future
COGNITIVE	think in the 'here and now' curious, energetic and eager learners	concrete thinking can identify and classify keen on rules, but little abstract thinking	think more logically and abstractly, but not always in relation to self	thinking more abstract – can distinguish real and concrete from abstract and possible
SELF	egocentric attitude 'me, my and mine' high self-esteem allows new tasks to be mastered	can describe themselves on several competencies more internally controlled	strong drive for autonomy, but still dependent very self-conscious	identify through exploring different roles – more time spent alone
SOCIAL	play is important associate with peers but can misunderstand each other	peers very important, best friend and group membership values and beliefs beginning to emerge	strong need for peer approval makes them vulnerable	peers remain important – friendships more stable and mature

FIGURE 2.1 Child and adolescent development

EARLY CHILDHOOD	Pre-schoolers can face difficulties in their play with other children. They have a limited understanding of 'give and take'. They can become fearful through taking things literally. Being told that nanna has 'gone to sleep' when she has died, can make them fearful of bedtimes. A boy became frightened of going home because he was going to meet his new 'half brother'. How young children process emotional events shapes their reactions.
MIDDLE CHILDHOOD	At this age children become concerned about peer relationships, being chosen last for the team, being teased. There is a fear of losing friends, of not being liked by the teacher or being punished. Their increasing physical maturity means that physical appearance can be a source of anxiety. (In addition to these common worries, some children will be struggling with family breakdown, abusive relationships and poverty.)
EARLY ADOLESCENCE	Overwhelming feelings and a lack of ability to deal with them leads to anger and moodiness. Being oversensitive means that any relationship difficulties can be over-reacted to. They can be loving and caring one minute towards parents but quickly change to being hostile and rejecting. Their need for increased autonomy leads to resistance to authority figures – at home and in school.
MID-ADOLESCENCE	While mood swings lessen, there is pressure on relationships, which may be sexual in nature, and this increases the adolescents' anxiety. They can feel confused about their career choices and while they want more control, this can produce ambivalent feelings. Mixed feelings of elation and depression are not uncommon. Relationships at home can remain pressurised as the young person pushes for increased autonomy.

FIGURE 2.2 Child and adolescent challenges

The two fundamental questions to ask when working to design a behaviour programme are these:

1   What skills does the child need to deal effectively with the challenges she or he will face?
2   How can these skills be taught?

This gives us a simple but elegant solution matrix (see Figure 2.3).

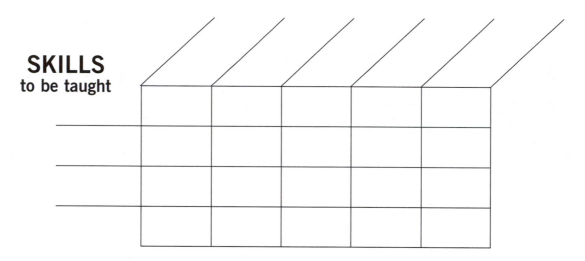

FIGURE 2.3 Outline of the solution intervention matrix

Interventions

Skills

What are the skills children need to cope with stress? (Notice our intention is not to eliminate stress but to enable children to cope more effectively with it.) Once we have established the skills we can now ask, 'How can these skills be taught?'

Emotional literacy
Emotional literacy is the individual's ability to experience and have the necessary skills to manage his or her emotions.

How can we develop emotional literacy skills?

1. Increase the vocabulary

Using pictures and photographs helps children to recognise and label different facial expressions and body postures.

2. Identify reactions and triggers

List situations that cause specific emotions. Show TV soap clips that allow children to predict, 'What will happen next?' What feelings were triggered?

3. Mood management

Using music, jokes and film clips helps children to learn to change what they are feeling by providing a trigger that is already associated with positive feelings.

Thinking skills

The way we think about things frequently causes more problems than the way things are in reality. False, irrational thoughts lead to stress. There are recognised 'thinking traps' that we fall into: we 'awfulise' things; we worry about things that never happen; we follow rules that are impossible to be successful at; we believe we 'should' be liked by everyone.

How can we develop thinking skills?

1. Thought-challenging

Together with the child produce some negative statements such as: 'I am unattractive'; 'I am stupid'; 'Nothing I try ever works out'; 'To be liked by people I must always please them'. (Doing this with the child removes the pressure from him or her. Asking children for their own negative statements can be too threatening.)

Teach the child the critical questions:

1   Does the thought seem sensible or silly?
2   Is it a helpful thought?
3   What would a friend say about the thought?
4   What would you tell a friend who had the same thought?

2. The worry box

With the child list all the common worries that you and other people have and create a 'worry box' from, for example, a shoebox. This is where worries that will not go away are to be put. Write or draw the child's worries with him or her and put them into the box. If at the end of the week they are still causing worry the child can be encouraged to talk them over with a parent, friend or school staff.

3. Success-thinking

Children often take a challenge, play it forward in their mind and see themselves failing. For example, even before a test children can be worrying about the reaction of their parents if they were to fail. Practise going through the situation with them. Where are they? Who are they with? How are they feeling? Rehearse a successful outcome. What are they thinking? What are other people saying? What can they say?

Self-care

Self-care is about developing a positive lifestyle that helps us move towards our goals.

How can we develop self-care skills?

1. Eating

Provide information to help children understand the importance of a balanced diet. Teach the link between good eating and good health.

2. Exercise

Any form of exercise that strengthens muscles and provides some cardiovascular fitness is an important aspect of self-care.

3. Sleep

While we all differ in the amount of sleep we need, for children and young people it can be some nine hours. Encourage regular routines around bed times. Avoiding big late-night meals and excessive caffeine will also help.

Active relaxation

Relaxation is an underestimated weapon against stress. Passive relaxation will just be time out in front of the TV, which is helpful for a time but not as effective as active relaxation, which is about learning definite strategies to cope with stress. Active relaxation involves an understanding of how stress triggers physiological responses that are preparing us for 'fight or flight'. Usually neither of these responses is appropriate; they just hype up our nervous system with energy that goes unused. Relaxation can be a powerful antidote to stress because we cannot be both aroused and relaxed at the same time.

How can we develop relaxation skills?

1. Progressive muscle relaxation

With the child or young person practise tensing muscle groups, shoulders, arms, etc. Hold them as tense as you can and then let all the tension out. Focus on the difference between the two conditions, tensed and relaxed. You could make an audio tape or CD for the child to use at home.

2. Controlled breathing

Help the child to practise breathing in deeply through the nose to the count of seven and then out through the mouth to the count of eleven. Deep breathing blocks the tendency to hyperventilate under stress.

3. Visualisation – with anchors

Encourage the child to choose a memory that has good feelings about it and to focus on the following questions. Where you are? Who are you with? What can you see? What can you smell? What are you wearing? What feelings do you have? Now the child should cross his or her fingers and keep practising getting in touch with the memory, especially the positive feelings, with the crossing of fingers. The more the child does it the easier it becomes to feel those good feelings whenever he or she wishes to.

Social support

Because we are social animals we each need some degree of time with those we care for and who care for us. Relationships are central to our identity. Every role we have assumes that there is someone else there: a father needs a child; a wife needs a husband; a teacher needs a learner; a writer needs a reader; a boy needs a girl. Our family and friends enable us to cope with stressful situations. The more isolated children are the less well they will cope. A buddy system can help link isolated children into their peer group.

1. Time

Making time to be with children or young people can provide them with the opportunity to explore worries that they have. Talking through concerns allows them to consider various options and is also a reality check: 'This is bothering me. Should it?'

2. Buddy system
Allocating older peers who have some training in basic listening skills can be a positive resource for children who may find talking to an adult threatening or overwhelming.

3. Support map
Help children to list all the people in their lives. What are the qualities and skills they possess? Who would they go to with different kinds of worries? Encourage them to practise seeking help, rather than passively waiting for it. If you fell into a hole it would be useful to shout so that people know you need help rather than just sitting and waiting for someone to happen by.

We can now begin to develop the solution matrix outlined in Figure 2.3. As you can see in Figure 2.4 we now have a range of interventions that can be placed across the top axis. The vertical axis comprises those areas in which the child or young person lacks specific skills. When we need to develop an individual programme the matrix can act as a simple but effective *aide mémoire*.

Problem-solving skills

Behaviour is adaptive and functional and aims to increase a child's chance of survival. Problem behaviours are usually attempts to solve problem situations.

It is easy to say that most children lack the necessary developmental skills to solve problems. Our challenge within the educational context is to teach them those skills. Even if we only teach them to –

STOP	What is the problem?
THINK	What are possible solutions?
	What are the outcomes to different choices?
CHOOSE	Is it a good choice or bad choice in terms of the outcomes?

– it is a beginning. This chapter explores a range of ideas to strengthen our commitment to teaching children problem-solving skills.

While most children naturally develop problem-solving skills, there are some who, for a number of reasons, fail to do so. Children who use them are more popular with their peers and receive more positive feedback from adults. They seem to be able to regulate their own behaviour through having such skills as:

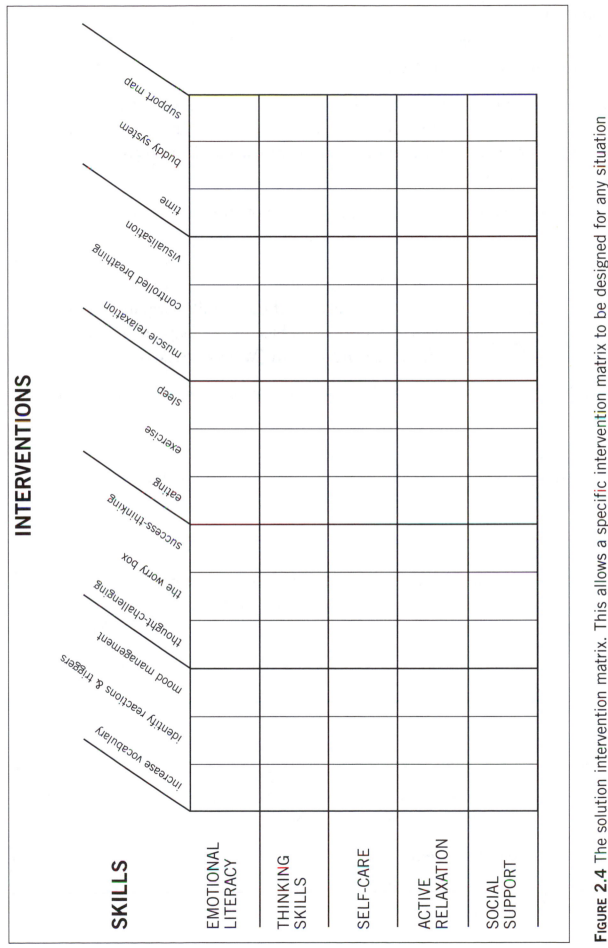

INTERVENTIONS

increase vocabulary
identify reactions & triggers
mood management
thought-challenging
the worry box
success-thinking
eating
exercise
sleep
muscle relaxation
controlled breathing
visualisation
time
buddy system
support map

SKILLS

EMOTIONAL LITERACY

THINKING SKILLS

SELF-CARE

ACTIVE RELAXATION

SOCIAL SUPPORT

FIGURE 2.4 The solution intervention matrix. This allows a specific intervention matrix to be designed for any situation

- foreseeing outcomes
- delaying their responses
- monitoring their own behaviour.

Children who have learning difficulties or suffer with attention deficit and hyperactivity find mastering such skills hard. They benefit from having problem-solving skills broken down into the component parts and being given opportunities to over-learn.

Many adults see these skills as being at the core of children becoming responsible citizens. Children's successful development into adulthood and into democratic society is dependent on their ability to use critical judgement, effective decision-making skills and perspective-taking, regardless of their innate ability and cultural or family background. The teaching of these skills early in life can serve to protect against or prevent the onset of problem behaviours such as drug abuse, pregnancy, school dropout, suicide and so forth (Webster-Stratton, 1999).

When we are trying to help children and young people solve problems we are doing two things at the same time:

1   Helping them to recognise when they have a problem.
2   Teaching them how to make decisions and generate possible solutions.

Techniques

> An ordinary person almost never approaches a problem systematically and exhaustively unless he has been specifically educated to do so.
>
> (Miller, 1960)

There are essentially three types of problem-solving techniques: convergent, divergent and lateral.

Convergent

Convergent thinking is when we use a systematic, linear approach. We follow a set of predetermined steps. Typically these are:

STEP 1: Define the problem.
STEP 2: Think of possible solutions.
STEP 3: Choose a solution.

STEP 4: What will help you to use this solution?

STEP 5: What will hinder you from using this solution?

STEP 6: Can you live with this solution?

STEP 7: What will be the gains from solving this problem?

STEP 8: How will you reward yourself?

Convergent problem-solving is a logical and deliberate approach to solving problems. It moves slowly but determinedly towards a solution. It is the approach most used in scientific investigations. These steps are explored in fuller detail on p. 36.

Divergent

Divergent thinking is far less structured and tends to be more creative. It draws on intuition, innovation, visualisation, humour and the absurd. This approach encourages spontaneity. As Caroselli (1997) puts it, 'The creative approach diverges from the straight-and-narrow path that convergent thinking requires you to follow.'

Otherwise known as the *Janusian technique* after the Roman god of beginnings and endings (Janus), the technique encourages thinking from two different directions. It involves asking a range of questions that tease out what will help us to succeed and what will lead to failure.

Write the problem down.

STEP 1: Ask these success-oriented questions.
● Who could most likely solve this problem?
● How have similar problems been solved?
● What skills are needed to solve this problem?

STEP 2: Ask these failure-oriented questions.
● Who could least likely solve this problem?
● How have similar problems not been solved?
● What skills have not been used to solve this problem?

Lateral thinking

The most successful problem-solvers are those who are able to use both approaches: lateral thinkers. While a game of football follows clear rules, and success is clearly defined by scoring a goal, there is considerable flexibility within the rules for the lateral thinker to be creative. Lateral thinkers are able to choose the problem-solving approach that is most suitable in any given set of circumstances. It should be noted that the convergent approach is close to decision-making, that is, following logical steps to come to a rational plan of action. Repairing a bike puncture, for example, involves a limited number of choices and our thinking is likely to be sequential. Any other reasonable person would have made similar decisions. Deciding what to play at lunchtime, on the other hand, involves holding in mind many different possible outcomes and using divergent thinking.

But we are not just rational beings – we are also irrational, that is, what is psychologically rational to me is not necessarily to you. Problem-solving involves the person's feelings, preferences and values.

How do I know which approach to use?

The more skilled young people are in both convergent and divergent thinking skills the better equipped they are. We each have a preferred style, but this can at times be a weakness. It is best for young people to use a combination of methods in order for them to appreciate that problem-solving involves both the head and the heart.

Worked example of a convergent problem-solving approach by a child in school

STEP 1: Define the problem.
- The child sitting next to you plays with your hair, kicks you under the table and is generally annoying.

STEP 2: Think of possible solutions.
- Ask to be moved to another seat.
- Ask the child to stop doing it.
- Ask to have a meeting with the teacher and the child.
- Ask your Mum and Dad for help.

STEP 3: Choose a solution.

- Ask to meet with your teacher and the child to discuss matters.

STEP 4: What will help you use this solution?

- You get on well with the teacher.
- The teacher is aware that you are being distracted.

STEP 5: what will hinder you using this solution?

- The child will think you're a 'tell-tale'.

STEP 6: Can you live with this solution?

STEP 7: What will be the benefits of solving this problem?

- More work done.
- Get on better with the pupil.

STEP 8: How will you reward yourself?

- I will tell my parents that I successfully sorted a problem out.

Worked example of a divergent (Janusian) problem-solving approach by a child in school

Write the problem down.

Someone has been on the computer for a VERY long time and you have some work you need to do on it.

STEP 1: ask these success-oriented questions.

- Who could most likely solve this problem?
  Sharon.
- How have similar problems been solved?
  By going to the teacher.
  By telling the teaching assistant.
  By explaining to the pupil why you need the computer.
- What skills are needed to solve this problem?
  Assertiveness.
  Staying calm.
  Avoiding confrontation.
  Being determined.

STEP 2: Ask these failure-oriented questions.

- Who could least likely solve this problem?

  Ben.

- How have similar problems not been solved?

  There have been arguments about whose turn it is

  Not telling anyone about the problem.

- What skills have not been used to solve this problem?

  Politeness

  Compromise

  Patience.

Now write down three solutions to the problem.

- Explain my needs politely
- Arrange a time when I can have the computer
- Tell an adult the problem I'm having.

Core beliefs

As we will see in the final chapter, the way that we think plays a very significant part in determining how we feel and behave. As children develop they learn scripts that control their behaviour. Examples would be learning:

- to be a boy/girl
- about relationships
- about the kind of person you are.

These scripts become subconscious guides of behaviour. For most children they are, of course, positive. But there are occasions when they are negative. They can be about their learning ability, 'I'm thick', or about their friendships, 'Nobody will like me'.

Another example with troubled children is the development of negative expectations about how adults are going to behave towards them. These expectations will shape their behaviour. For example, it is not uncommon for children who come from difficult circumstances to be placed in foster homes. These placements often experience a 'honeymoon' period, but then matters deteriorate to the point that the placement breaks down. An explanation for this would be that the children have a deep-seated expectation of ultimately being rejected. To test this they push the boundaries with their behaviour until finally, and sadly, they are 'rejected'.

We can see that what inner self-belief does is create a self-fulfilling cycle:

- I am unlikeable
- so I behave nastily towards you
- so you don't like me
- which proves my point.

Children who experience harsh conditions are vulnerable to developing negative inner core beliefs. To discover their core beliefs there are two key questions:

1   What does the observable behaviour say about the child? We are inferring that the child has underlying beliefs that explain the behaviour. For example the child who avoids going out at playtimes and prefers to stay close to adults is likely to have such core beliefs as:

   I am unlikeable.
   I will be hurt.

2   What does the observable behaviour say about how the child thinks about other people? In the example of the withdrawn child it could be:

   people are nasty and hurtful.

Changing such strongly held assumptions is no easy task. But at least our model accepts that such beliefs do need to be addressed. Below are some practical ideas to help children and young people develop positive inner self-beliefs.

Evidence
Keep a diary or folder of *all* examples of evidence which goes against the core belief. This is important, as core beliefs will tend to find and exaggerate any evidence which supports them.

Alternative self-beliefs
Develop and strengthen new, alternative core beliefs. Working with the child, explore the examples of 'exceptions' found in the evidence-gathering exercise. How can some of these exceptions be explained:

- I can learn
- I am likeable

- I have good qualities
- I have the right to be wrong sometimes.

Using a diary or record form keep a log of all the examples that reinforce these beliefs.

Lifeline review

With the child or young person, produce a lifeline where all the events that support the new and positive core belief are detailed. The lifeline is a drawn line on a piece of paper with specific events placed in chronological order along it.

The above activities teach children how to look more positively at their lives. The techniques used are the antidote to the 'enemy within' that thrives on negativity. Without these skills all children are vulnerable to the pain of psychological thought-distortion.

Cognitive Behaviour Therapy

It's the thought that counts.

It is now that we return to some of the points that were made in the Introduction. The difficulties faced by children today are as great as ever.

The world has changed a lot for children in the past 50 years. In the past, children were positively socialised by the family, the community and the church as well as by school. Today, with the decreased influence of the community and the church, there is increased pressure on both parents and schools to socialise children so that they become respectful adults and citizens. An old African proverb comes to mind: 'It takes an entire village to raise one child.'

There does seem to have been an increase in negative forces acting on children. The extended family which used to support children and their parents is less in evidence today. The media often exposes children to issues ahead of their maturational ability to deal positively with them. Sadly children are often seen to be the cause of their problems rather than the victims. Seligman (1996) talks of an epidemic of pessimism. He believes that these negative forces have led to adults and children becoming trapped in negative attitudes and he challenges us to teach children how to be optimistic.

Clearly most children are not negative, depressed and cynical. They have similar values and belief systems to their parents. However, within the school context most teachers and support staff will have come across those children who seem to lack any desire to try to learn.

If we look at basic human development we can see that we are all prone to negative self-beliefs – beliefs which, if we allowed them free rein, would destroy our best efforts with cynical remarks and hurtful putdowns. The reason for this stems from our early experiences. Children are surrounded by adults as well as older siblings who seem capable of everything. They feel their dependency and are emotionally saddened and embarrassed by it. They all, then, have an inferiority complex. But while most children learn to accept and achieve within their potential, there are others who become trapped by their fear of failure. The best way such children safeguard the little self-esteem that they have is not to try at all. Most school staff can quickly name those learners who, if they would only try a little harder, could make significant progress. But their learning is held back by their fear of getting it wrong and, because they are caged in by a deep-seated expectation of failure, trying seems pointless. The biggest enemy to the success of many children is within them, rather than being outside factors or experiences.

The negative inner dialogue

We all have an internal dialogue with ourselves. Many young people learn an inner script in an atmosphere of insecurity, which quickly becomes an automatic negative script that is a mental block to future learning. An example might be:

> *I've never done this before. I am going to get it wrong. The others will do it easily. I will look stupid. I won't try.*

The script we want is as follows:

> *I've never done this before. I might get it wrong. Everybody makes mistakes. I will try. That's how I will learn to get it right.*

Optimism – the Seligman way

At the core of this approach – which is common to several other theories – is the link between thoughts and feelings. It is the way that we interpret events that leads us to feel in certain ways. The more we practise particular thinking styles, the more we think in that way. It is easier for the optimist to see the positive because she or he is well practised at it. Equally the pessimist has had plenty of practice in seeing problems.

This model is quite naturally of value to those children and young people who are able to engage in discussion about their thinking styles. It will not be suitable for all children and we need to have approaches that help children who are vulnerable to 'getting their thinking in a knot'. The earlier we can teach them core skills the less likely they are to dig their own thinking traps.

These approaches can be summed up by the saying quoted at the beginning of this chapter: 'It's the thought that counts'. This is the core principle of Cognitive Behaviour Therapy. It is not a quick-fix, magical cure. It works if people work at it.

The core skills are:

1   Thought-catching
2   Evaluating
3   Pursuing accurate alternatives.

Ellis (1962) and Beck (1979), the founders of Cognitive Behaviour Therapy, developed the ABC model which is summarised below.

The ABC model

A is the *activating event* – the trigger. The trigger can be one of many things, and there are different triggers for different people. Triggers relate to the situations that we are in: at home, in the classroom or in the playground. In the playground, for example, not being chosen to join in a game can act as a trigger to either anxiety or anger. However, there are common triggers that tend often, although not necessarily, to set off the same types of thought in different people. Spotting the trigger can give the first clue to the difficulties a young person may be struggling with.

B stands for the *beliefs* held about the event. Certain events will automatically awaken certain beliefs, which are not always conscious. This part of the cycle has often been left out in the past because beliefs can be deep-rooted in our subconscious minds and we respond to them unknowingly. But it is the belief that determines how we respond to the event. The child who has experienced success will believe new learning situations are positive opportunities, whereas a child who has struggled and failed repeatedly will try to avoid such situations.

(Such beliefs have been found to exist within institutions as well as individuals, for example in the case of institutional racism, to which we could also add sexism and disability discrimination. The beliefs about these issues are socialised so deeply into us that we are unaware of them but they determine our feelings about and our attitudes to the world we live in. Often it takes someone with a different perspective to enable us to see them.)

C stands for the *consequences* – the feelings and the behaviours that follow the event. It is how we feel and what we do as a result of what we think. When a new child joins a class, if he or she believes that others will like and treat him or her kindly, the child displays feelings of positive anticipation and friendly behaviours towards new peers.

A negative example of the ABC model is as follows. Dean is pushed by another student in the playground. This trigger (A – activating event) leads straight to Dean's core belief (B) that people are 'out to do him down'. As a result he feels angry, becomes physiologically aroused and hits out at the student (C – consequences).

This example clearly links all of the core systems within the student and explains the outcomes in psychologically 'rational' terms. Even though the consequences are irrational, in that they do not help Dean cope effectively with his world, they follow his beliefs. An understanding of this model will enable us to teach students appropriate skills to take control and change their pre-programmed response patterns.

We are now in a position to produce some ABC templates which link antecedents, beliefs and consequences closely to each other. As the examples below indicate, the triggers could be anything and everything. For example, let's picture three students who have all failed an exam:

- Adela is angry because a week before the exam she was told that her tutor had not covered the entire syllabus.
- Randeep is anxious because he is going to have tell his parents and he is not sure how they will react.
- Dawn is indifferent. She did not work for the exam and she has already secured a job that she wants to do.

In the above examples the trigger leads to these consequences because of the way in which it is interpreted – it is the interpretation of the trigger that is all important, not the trigger itself. If people define things as being real, then the consequences will be real. If you believe walking under a ladder is bad luck it matters not what the truth is – you behave 'as if' it were true.

Template 1. The ABC of anger

Activating event (trigger)
- being teased
- being pushed
- being left out
- family changes

Beliefs (interpretation)
- must get even
- must not let them push me around
- they're always picking on me

Consequences

Emotional reaction
- hating
- angry
- hurt
- revengeful

Behavioural reaction
- fighting
- arguing
- breaking things

Physiological arousal
- sweating
- increased heart rate
- fast breathing

Template 2. The ABC of anxiety

Activating event (trigger)
- unexpected changes
- speaking in public
- meeting new people

Beliefs (interpretation)
- I can't cope
- I will look stupid
- people will laugh at me

Consequences

Emotional reaction
- helpless
- nervous
- scared

Behavioural reaction
- withdrawn
- isolated
- passive
- dependent

Physiological arousal
- increased blood pressure
- sweating
- shaking

Template 3. The ABC of depression

Activating event (trigger)
- unexpected failure
- bereavement
- family changes

Beliefs (interpretation)
- life is just not fair
- I can't cope without them
- nobody cares about me

Consequences

Emotional reaction
- sad
- unsure
- lonely

Behavioural reaction
- inactive
- sulking
- withdrawn

Physiological arousal
- low energy
- low activity
- poor appetite

What is to be done?

The model we have now developed builds positively on our previous chapters. Instead of stress-proofing and problem-solving being discrete approaches they are brought together more coherently. Each approach plays an important role in helping children and young people take control. If our interventions were not always successful in the past it may have been because we were not using a multifaceted approach. To use a medical analogy: being given the correct medicine is part of the solution, but not all of it; the patient also needs a healthy diet and a supportive environment.

The difficulties that children face are rarely caused by one discrete factor. They are usually multidimensional and have negative influences in all aspects of a child's development. It follows, then, that we need a multiple response plan. It is no good trying to change a child's behaviour if the thoughts that gave rise to the behaviour remain in place.

In our efforts to help children and young people cope effectively this model lifts the fog. We have for too long been sold the idea that there is *one* approach that is the right and only way. If only life were that simple! The truth is that we have different models and approaches because we are by nature complex. Our interventions need to be broad-based – Cognitive Behaviour Therapy enables us to take the best from each approach.

Cognitive Behaviour Therapy involves change in the following areas:

1   Taking control of the physiological arousal
2   Challenging the thinking
3   Practising alternative responses/behaviour.

Any programme to help a student take control of a problem will involve techniques from each of the three areas listed above.

Our model is represented in Figure 2.5.

Having covered two of the intervention areas, thinking and relaxation, we now have the third piece of the jigsaw to solve – behaviour.

Behavioural interventions

The behavioural approach stemmed from the pioneering work of such people as Pavlov, Watson and Skinner. It was a reaction to the psychoanalytic

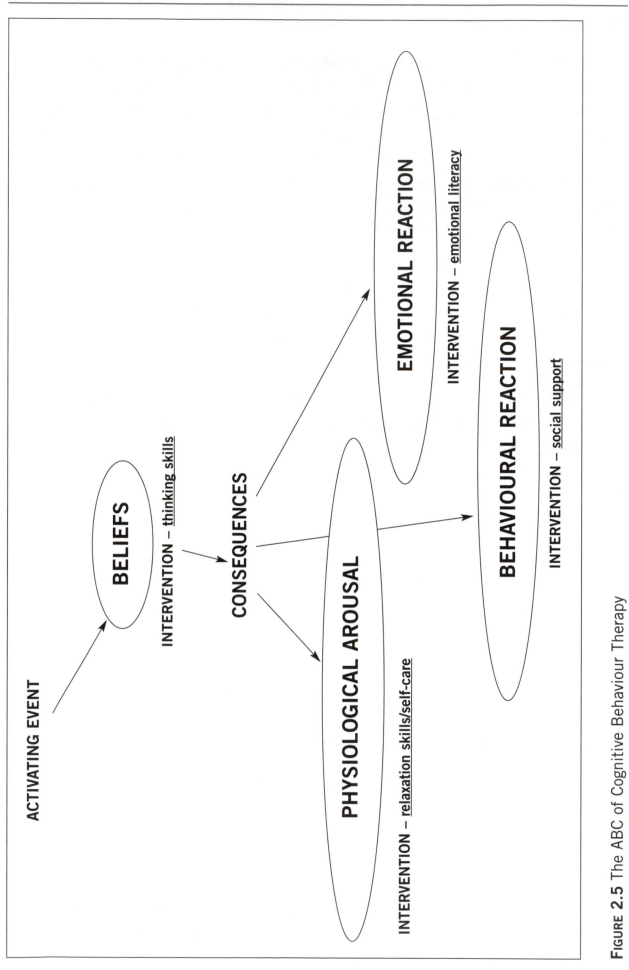

ACTIVATING EVENT

BELIEFS

INTERVENTION – <u>thinking skills</u>

CONSEQUENCES

EMOTIONAL REACTION

INTERVENTION – <u>emotional literacy</u>

PHYSIOLOGICAL AROUSAL

INTERVENTION – <u>relaxation skills/self-care</u>

BEHAVIOURAL REACTION

INTERVENTION – <u>social support</u>

FIGURE 2.5 The ABC of Cognitive Behaviour Therapy

interpretation of behaviour as purported by Freud. The emphasis in this approach is more on overt behaviour than on thoughts and feelings.

In the school setting we are often faced by children who show an excess of particular behaviours, such as leaving their seat, shouting out and distracting others. It is easy to turn to behavioural techniques to control and reduce such behaviours. This is an eliminative approach; it focuses on the problem behaviour and removes it through such techniques as:

- *extinction*, which is removing the link between a specific behaviour and its consequence
- and *punishment*, which is the prevention of a behaviour by its association with an unpleasant outcome.

While such approaches may appear satisfactory for school staff, there is a far preferable one: the educative approach. Behavioural techniques have come a long way, and are now used extensively in support of other approaches, but here the assessment is more on what the child needs to do, rather than on what s/he should not to do. The orientation is towards constructing rather than eliminating behavioural repertoires, and our much more positive educational aim is to expand rather than contract what the child can do. Through increasing children's behavioural repertoires we are increasing their freedom as well as their positive adjustment to the school environment.

The eliminative approach does improve children's adjustment to their environment, but through restriction rather than expansion. For these reasons the techniques described highlight those approaches that increase a child's repertoire of behaviours.

The core principle of the behavioural approach is that behaviour is adaptive to immediate rewards and punishments. The child who is fearful of being rejected, for example, is over-clinging towards his or her carers. This leads to the adult carers being negative and punishing the child, which makes the child fear rejection and cling even more. The very behaviour the adults are trying to correct is in fact being maintained by them.

When a child has become used to a certain pattern of responses to his or her behaviour and an adult decides to break the pattern – 'I will no longer give you attention for that behaviour' – the child's behaviour often becomes worse. There is an 'extinction tantrum' through which the child attempts to force the pre-existing rewards to start again. If this process is not understood adults can give up using the right intervention; but the fact that the behaviour gets worse shows that the intervention is working.

Behavioural techniques and principles

- *Positive reinforcement.* Allow the child to earn a rewarding event/object/activity after the desired behaviour.
- *Observational learning.* Provide opportunities for the child to see a peer carry out the behaviour and receive a reward.
- *Chaining.* The reward can only be obtained after more than one example of the desired behaviour has been performed in succession. Gradually more examples of the behaviour are required to obtain the reward.
- *Role rehearsal.* The child may have some of the necessary skills but not the entire repertoire. A hierarchy of skills is developed and the child's behaviour is shaped through successive approximations to the desired behaviour.
- *Social-skills training.* Coaching is provided to enable the child to learn such skills as sharing, listening, turn-taking and co-operating with peers.

To bring these different techniques together refer back to the solution intervention matrix (Figure 2.4). Whenever a child or young person has areas of concern draw on all five sets of techniques:

1 Emotional literacy
2 Thinking skills
3 Self-care
4 Active relaxation
5 Social support.

This will increase the likelihood of success. Using techniques from just one area will reduce the chances of success. Why?

- Because multifaceted problems need multifaceted solutions.

Case example

Winston is 11 years old and plays inappropriately with peers: he can be excessively friendly, and then aggressive when peers reject his 'friendship'. In class he works well when supported, but otherwise he will wander around the class disrupting other children until he is reprimanded and made to return to his seat – where he receives support.

Interventions

The interventions put in place for Winston are shown in the programme planner (Figure 2.6). Time and adult support were required for him to learn the necessary new skills. But, little by little, the interventions produced positive results.

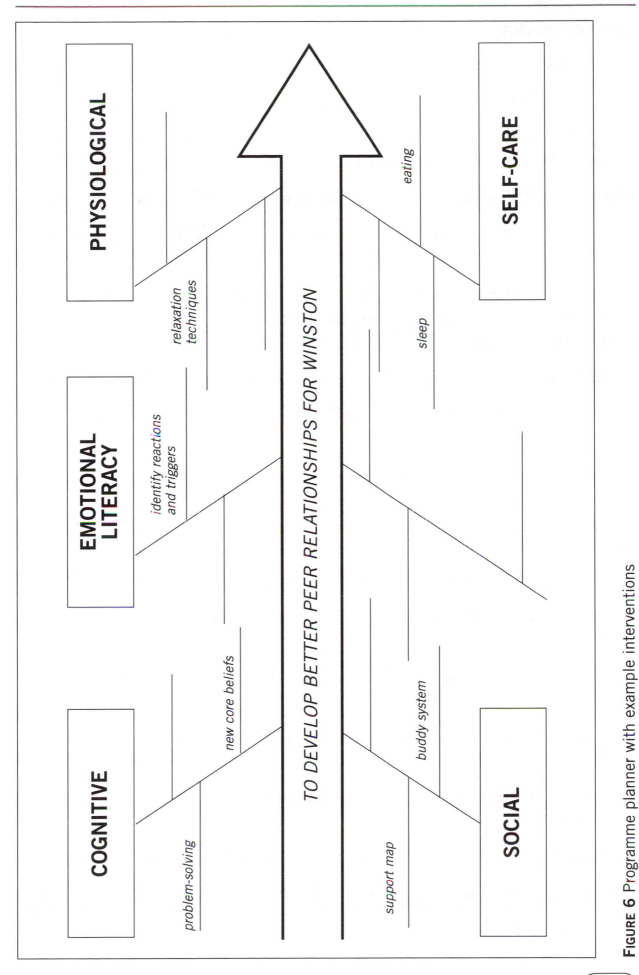

FIGURE 6 Programme planner with example interventions

Further reading

References

Beck, A. (1979) *Cognitive therapy for depression*. New York: Guildford Press.

Caroselli, M. (1997) *That's No Problem: a problem-free approach to problem solving*. West Des Marlene: American Media Incorporated.

Ellis, A. (1962) *Reason and emotion in psychotherapy*. New York: Lyle-Stewart.

Emerson, C. (2001) *Pressures in UK health care*. London: The Institute for Fiscal Studies.

Harold, G., Pryor J., and Reynolds, J. (2001) *Not in front of the children: how conflict between parents affects children*. London: One Plus One Marriage & Partnership Research.

Miller, G. (1960) *Plans and the structure of behaviour*. New York: R. & W. Holt.

Seligman, M. (1996) *The Optimistic Child*. New York: Harper Perennial.

Webster-Stratton, C. (1999) *How to promote children's social and emotional competence*. London: Paul Chapman.

Recommended reading

Eriksson, S. (2001) *On Football*. Italy: Carlton Books.

Greenberger, D. and Padesky, C. (1995) *Mind over mood*. New York: The Guilford Press.

Herbert, M. (1981) *Behavioural Treatment of Problem Children*. London: Academic Press.

Langelier, C. (2001) *Mood Management*. Thousand Oaks, USA: Sage Publications.

Langelier, C. (2001) *Mood Management: leader's manual*. Thousand Oaks, USA: Sage Publications.

McNamara, S. (2000) *Stress in young people*. London: Continuum.

Muller, D., Harris, P. and Wattley, L. (1987) *Nursing Children*. London: Harper & Row.

Nelson-Jones, R. (1983) *Practical Counselling Skills*. London: Holt, Rinehart & Winston.

O'Rourke, K. and Worzbyt, J. (1996) *Support groups for children*. USA: Accelerated Development.

Robertson, S. (2001) *Problem solving*. East Sussex: Psychology Press.

Scotti, J. and Meyer, L. (1999) *Behavioural Intervention*. Baltimore: Brookes.

Stallard, P. (2002) *Think Good – Feel Good*. Chichester: John Wiley & Sons.

 **Children's Thoughts and Feelings**

Introduction

There are no fixed measures to help us say whether a child's behaviour is abnormal, but the more extreme a child's behaviour is, the easier it becomes to do so. The label 'emotional, social and behavioural difficulties' (SEBD) has become synonymous with behaviours that prevent a child from successfully engaging with the curriculum and with his or her peers. That is to say, there are certain circumstances when the child's behaviour is different enough from that of his or her peers to justify additional adult intervention. Children who experience SEBD interfere in some way with the teacher's teaching, their peers' learning and their own learning. 'SEBD' is then more a description of a set of circumstances than a fixed diagnosis. A child's behaviour (for example, shouting out) may be of concern in one context – the classroom – but be perfectly normal in another – the playground.

Most of our understanding about the challenges that children face in schools stems from our knowledge of their social and behavioural development. Less has been written about children's emotional development and how problems in this complex process can result in barriers to children engaging with the curriculum.

This chapter aims to explain:

- the nature and function of emotions
- the underlying causes of emotional conflicts
- the nature of maladaptive coping mechanisms
- why boys tend to 'act out' and girls tend to 'act in'
- interventions to promote the use of adaptive coping styles.

Many children respond to inner emotional conflicts by behaving in ways that may be inappropriate or destructive. Any behaviour which occurs sufficiently often can become an over-learned response. When children face problems they naturally try to solve them; however, their solution can be a problem to others.

The information offered here will help school staff understand students' behaviours within the classroom. It will provide practical guidance for those staff who at times work either with small groups or in a one-to-one situation. When we are trying to alter a student's patterns of behaviour we should have both good reasons and a sound model for the interventions we put in place.

The model which is at the heart of this chapter is based on the writings of Robert Plutchik (Plutchik, 2000).

Our biology

We first need to appreciate that our physical make-up provides us with basic primary emotions which exist to help keep us alive. This is because the lower part of our brain evolved to survive in the jungle and ensured that we respond to threats by 'fight or flight'. The emotions we are born with are fear, joy, surprise, anger, disgust and curiosity. These are believed to be innately patterned responses to certain stimuli and enable us to interact successfully with our environment. The negative emotions of fear, anger and disgust help to motivate us to avoid dangers, while the positive emotions of joy, surprise and curiosity help us to explore our world. If we still lived in the jungle these emotions would be very adaptive for our survival.

The basic biological needs that we all have are:

- to survive
- to be nurtured
- to give nurture
- to reproduce.

Because we live in society we have developed higher emotions that help us to live together. Some of these are guilt and embarrassment. Babies have no sense of embarrassment about their bodily functions. But as they learn 'how to be' they experience shame and guilt. Without our social world there would be no emotional, social or behavioural difficulties. It is through socialisation that we all learn to judge ourselves by the standards of those who care for us. We see ourselves through their eyes.

A definition of emotions

Emotions are difficult to define because they cannot be observed directly, although we can sometimes see changes in a child's behaviour, or children can describe in words what they are feeling. At minimum, emotions are *the subjective experience of physiological arousal*. When a balloon suddenly bursts our heart rate increases, our breathing quickens and we experience the same bodily changes as with fear. The experience is also shaped by our thoughts. The fact that we saw that it was a balloon and not a gun that caused the noise influences our reaction. Our emotional responses are then a combination of innate physiological responses and our intellectual understanding of the situation.

The same physiological arousal can be experienced very differently. For example, the adrenaline rush from a roller-coaster ride might be as high as when we realise one of our children has gone missing and we search frantically for him or her – but the emotions we feel will be altogether different.

The way we interpret events shapes our emotional experience. Thinking that we were not invited to the party because of the exams we are about to take softens the pain of rejection. The pain exists, but it is understood differently.

Emotions are very complicated things and we can also experience different emotions at the same time. If a close friend moves away, for example, the sadness of his or her leaving is tinged with anger at being left behind.

Emotional development in children

Most children will successfully pass the stages briefly outlined below. When children face difficulties in a particular stage there can be negative effects that can influence the way in which they pass through a later stage. The model is similar to the construction of a house. If the foundation is not sound, then no matter how impressive the top floor looks it is not entirely secure.

Children's emotional competences increase with age and experience. The first stage is the attachment phase and begins at birth. During this phase children learn trust and a sense of belonging through experience (for example, their mother feeds them when they are hungry and cuddles them when they are upset). The challenge for them in this first stage is to be able to separate from their carer. At this early stage separation anxiety is observed and is at its strongest in the 18-month-old child. However, providing the child has experienced safe and loving relationships with her carer and the separation takes place in familiar surroundings where she is able to show a degree of independence, she is able readily to overcome this fear.

The next stage is the development of a sense of self. At around 18 months infants begin to understand that they are separate from their carers. They can now recognise themselves in the mirror and photographs. They have a sense of what is theirs and they enjoy successes as they overcome such challenges as learning to walk. During this stage the child has a strong 'me do it' attitude.

As they enter the toddler stage, by around two years old, they begin to enjoy social interaction with peers. They engage in what is called parallel play, tending to play alongside rather than interacting actively with their peers. They relate best to one adult at a time.

In middle childhood (approximately four to eleven years old) they are well able to follow daily routines. They can both respect and understand basic rules, though they can be rather fixed in following rules blindly as if they cannot be changed. Emotionally they are well able to show affection and they display a wide range of emotional reactions appropriate to different situations. They are empathic towards others and will offer comfort to others in distress.

Negative effects of difficulties during a developmental stage

A degree of emotional damage is illustrated by Chi, who is five years old and cared for by a father who is cold, distant and insensitive to his needs. Chi seeks to obtain love in very unloving and unlovable ways. He swings from being over-affectionate to people he hardly knows, to biting and breaking their toys. Children like Chi often develop poor peer relationships, experience learning difficulties and find it hard to maintain relationships. Chi will often hug other children so hard that they cry; when they avoid playing with him, he hits out at them.

How do emotions help us?

At a very basic level they help us to go towards those things that are good for us and to avoid those that might harm us. Disgust is a good example. Any food that is associated with potential harm becomes difficult to eat. Watching infants being offered food that has a 'nasty' taste or smell proves this point – they will not eat it. (This is why many foods are described as an 'acquired' taste. We have to overcome our natural dislike of them.)

Emotions also communicate to others two important pieces of information. Firstly, my behaviour tells others something about how I am feeling: bared teeth indicate anger, for example. Secondly, they can inform others of the kind of behaviour that can be expected: my bared teeth warn of aggressive behaviours and that I might attack; passive behaviours such as hanging my head and avoiding eye contact may suggest that I need help.

While this is interesting, we do not live in the jungle. We are social animals that have acquired the ability to communicate through language and to develop incredibly complex and sophisticated cultures. How we should behave is not determined simply by the hard wiring of our biological inheritance. Ways of thinking and feeling that are culturally acceptable are mediated to us by our family. All children are socialised, learning which emotions are considered appropriate to express and which are not. These can be seen in the emotional 'tags' that we are given as children and that we carry with us all our lives. (This notion is explored further in Chapter 2.)

Conflicting emotions

After the age of about four, children start to hold back their spontaneous expression of emotions. They begin to control their emotions as a result of the myths they learn. Some of these include:

- big boys don't cry
- cheer up – have some chocolate
- grieve alone – hide your feelings
- you shouldn't feel like that
- be happy.

Children learn to avoid unpleasant negative emotions that can cause anxiety by developing 'defence mechanisms'. They may learn to distract themselves through keeping busy. They may be encouraged to cheer up, even though what they are feeling is a natural response. They may be given a reward – such as chocolate – for suppressing their true feelings.

Freud believed that to safeguard us from negative emotions we all employ defence mechanisms that help us to avoid reality and the pain that it could cause us. This concept is one of Freud's major, and most widely accepted, contributions to our understanding of child and adult behaviours. If defence mechanisms are used excessively, the child (or adult) never learns to face the challenge of reality.

Defence mechanisms and gender

There is a tendency for boys to respond in a different way from girls in the defence mechanisms they use to avoid negative emotions. The reasons for this may be summed up as follows:

- different hormones – boys are more predisposed biologically to 'act out' – attack as a means of defence
- language – girls acquire language earlier and have a wider emotional vocabulary to analyse their feelings
- social – girls are conditioned to avoid outward displays of anger and therefore 'act in'.

The use of defence mechanisms is explored below at p. 66.

The model

The model in Figure 3.1 can be described as a psychosocial evolutionary model. It incorporates our knowledge from three distinct disciplines: sociology, psychology and evolutionary biology.

1   Our biology provides us with emotions to help us survive.
2   Our society teaches us to avoid certain negative emotions.
3   Defence mechanisms develop as a way of helping us cope.
4   If we over-rely on defence mechanisms they become less effective.
5   Girls tend to use 'acting in' defences and boys tend to use 'acting out' defences.

Tags

As children grow within the family their feelings are shaped by the way in which their carers respond to them. A useful way of understanding this is to imagine carers giving children 'tags' to help them on their journey. These tags are charged with a sense of emotional correctness and, as children, we learn to want to live up to them. When we fail to do so we can often feel guilt, reflecting how close to the very core of our personal identity are these tags that are imposed on us. Some of the most common tags are listed below:

- be strong
- please others

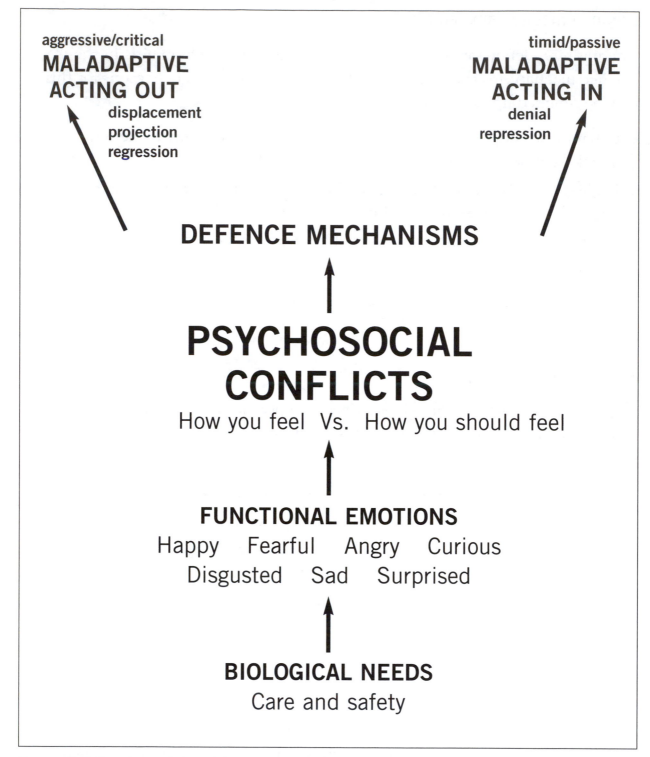

FIGURE 3.1 Psychosocial evolutionary model

- be perfect
- hurry up
- try hard.

These tags are readily recognised by us as adults and there is nothing wrong with any of them *per se*. They are helpful in that they enable us to fit in with our unique family. But they can become problems when children are blindly being driven by them. They will be a problem for any girl who seeks above all to please others – girls have as much right to please themselves as anyone. Disabled children who have the tag 'be strong' will feel that they should never ask for assistance. They, like the rest of us, sometimes need support, but they can be socialised into suppressing their weaknesses for fear of being different from others. This reflects the past approach that people with disabilities should be 'normalised'. The assumption was that disabled people would really like to be 'normal' – therefore being given this tag was thought to be of value on their journey into the 'able-bodied' world.

The nature of 'tags'

- they can be definite assets to the individual
- they can cause problems when taken to extremes
- they can be changed through conscious effort.

When we are working with children who face specific challenges we need to be aware of the tags that might be guiding their behaviour. When appropriate, we can help them to understand both the strengths that their tags give them and also the weaknesses that can accompany them. The more insight children can gain the more likely they are to be able to take control of their behaviour. When this is not possible there are also some useful techniques by which we can help them respond more positively to the challenges they face. These relate to the ways in which we respond to them and are presented in the five tag templates below.

Tag template 1   Be strong

Asset to the child
'Be strong' children tend to be self-sufficient and require minimum help. They are hard-working and very willing to help others. They have a 'get on with it' attitude.

Liability for the child
These children can find relationships difficult. They would like to be cared for and supported but carry within them a fear of rejection. They find it very difficult to ask for help, either practical or emotional. This can make them appear somewhat lonely, cold and aloof towards others.

Personal challenge

The personal challenge for these children is to learn to ask for support as well as to take it. They need support in seeing their weaknesses as strengths. If learners understand that making mistakes and being helped to correct them is the normal way we all learn they will be more willing to seek help. Increasing their emotional insight and vocabulary through an understanding that other children have similar weaknesses to themselves can help them to share more of their feelings and not to fear rejection from others.

How to get the best out of 'be strong' children

Make sure you praise and acknowledge them for their consideration, kindness and determination. Do not over-push them to share their feelings but be prepared to model emotional literacy through talking about your own. At times allow them time to be alone.

Tag template 2   Please others

Asset to the child

Children who try hard to please others are very pleasant to be with. They join in, have generous natures and are more than willing to meet other people's needs and expectations. They are keen to follow rules – if, at times, a little obsessively.

Liability for the child

They can be prone to sudden outbursts of rudeness and bad temper as if they have become overloaded with a dislike of themselves for not being honest. This is passive aggression, meaning basically that they turn their negative feelings in on themselves. Occasionally the build-up of emotional tension can burst out towards others. These children can often feel that they are misunderstood and can display a 'holier than thou' attitude.

Personal challenge

The personal challenge for these children is to appreciate that they have a right to be themselves. They need to understand that their 'I don't mind' and 'if you like' manner can be extremely upsetting to close friends. Friends need them to be themselves – not simply to respond to everyone else's wishes as if they are following a rule book.

How to get the best out of 'please others' children
Respond positively to any authentic choices they make, and avoid giving responses which are clichés or patronising. Do not, for example, give praise for normal everyday events, choice of food, clothes or colours when painting ('That is a nice strong colour for the sky'). Thank them when they give honest replies to questions, especially when they express negative feelings – this is the one area that they probably have the most difficulties with.

Tag template 3   Be perfect

Asset to the child
'Be perfect' children have high standards in both their social and work life and are often very purposeful.

Liability for the child
They can be critical and non-accepting of others who have different standards. They are extremely self-critical and can be trapped into underachieving through not being able to submit work to a standard they think is good enough. They are prone to suffer anxiety and depression through excessive self-blame when things go wrong.

Personal challenge
'Be perfect' children have the task of accepting the fact that others have different standards from theirs, and to tolerate those whose standards fall short of their own but are equally valid. Encouraging such learners to review their work and to see what it is they have achieved can help avoid the feelings of sadness which comes from their only noticing their mistakes.

How to get the best out of 'be perfect' children
Often these children need reassurance that when things go wrong it is not necessarily their fault. It is good to tease them gently and to confront them, caringly, with the illogicality of their position.

Tag template 4   Hurry up

Asset to the child
'Hurry up' children tend to be fun, lively and adventurous. They are the embryonic form of your 'likeable rogue'. They are very sociable and enjoy attention.

Liability for the child
They can develop a 'devil may care' attitude and may become extreme risk takers in their personal and social lives, seeming to pay little heed to the potential dangers of their actions. They tend to have a need for immediate attention as and when they want it. They can seem to be self-destructive when overwhelmed by challenges and responsibilities.

Personal challenge
It can help if 'hurry up' children have set lists of what they are to achieve each day. This can help them put some structure and boundaries around their behaviour and is a useful way to help them limit the number of tasks they try to complete.

How to get the best out of 'hurry up' children
These children benefit from being praised for their efficiency. They need reassurance that there is plenty of time for their tasks. When they have outbursts and demand your attention, be firm but clear that you will attend to them when they are calmer and more rational. Enabling them to join school clubs where 'exciting' activities are properly supervised can be a positive move to curb their risk-taking behaviours. Care needs to be taken to ensure that they are only set small, manageable tasks to avoid overloading them and triggering negative self-destructive responses.

Tag template 5   Try hard

Asset to the child
'Try hard' children have commitment and can be very caring and supportive towards others who need help – especially the 'underdog'. They can be very passionate and persistent in any enterprise.

Liability for the child

'Try hard' children can be prone to inferiority complexes. They can be aggressive – though in their eyes they are being assertive. There is a danger that they can use others as scapegoats and blame them for their own failures.

Personal challenge

'Try hard' children need the confidence to risk both failing and succeeding. They need support and encouragement to stop saying they will 'try' but to adopt an 'I will' attitude.

How to get the best out of 'try hard' children

Through subtle and implicit ways show your faith in their ability to achieve set tasks and give them support to complete the tasks that they begin. Tactically ignore self-deprecating statements about themselves or others.

Personal note

If you change 'child' to 'adult' in each of the above tags you can see that they have equal relevance to all of us. We all have tags from our own childhood that remain within us throughout our lives. If we have no awareness of them they will lead us, sometimes, to where we don't wish to be. But if we are aware of them we can consciously use them to our advantage. Sometimes being strong is an asset to me; at other times it is a definite liability. I now realise that, when I ask for help, I am not showing how weak I am but how strong I have become.

It is not difficult to see that some tags relate closely to some of the defence mechanisms we are to consider in the next chapter. Children who have a 'be strong' tag, for example, will be likely to use avoidance or denial when faced with challenges that they feel unable to manage. The child with a 'be perfect' tag will be susceptible to overcompensating for his or her apparent weaknesses. The child with a 'try hard' tag may well project his or her own weaknesses on to others.

However, it is important to appreciate that, while the tags are acquired through early childhood experiences in the family, defence mechanisms become part of a child's emotional defence repertoire to protect him or her, in his or her interactions with the wider world. Most families have an open relationship with the outside world – they adapt and change through the feedback they receive. The more closed a family is in its relationships with the outside world, the more likely it is that the tags of the family members will be 'dysfunctional'. That is, they work in the family but not in wider society. Under such circumstances it is more likely that a child will develop maladaptive defence mechanisms.

Maladaptive defence mechanisms

As we saw in Chapter 1, children's ways of dealing with emotional conflicts vary. It is not hard to imagine the emotional distress so many children experience when, for whatever reason, they find that they are unable to do tasks that others find easy. The child with dyslexia is confused by the difficulty he or she finds with reading. The child with a hearing loss feels excluded from everyday conversations. And the child who cannot keep up physically with his or her peers feels different and left out. Children, like adults, use defence mechanisms to deal with the regrets, anxiety and conflicts that they experience. The most common defence mechanisms are:

- compensation – finding areas of strength to focus on enables the learner to obtain support and positive feedback from others; for example, issues of learning difficulties are avoided through being 'clever at art'

- regression – the learner uses infantile ways of expressing anxiety; for example, crying

- displacement – the releasing of negative emotional tension that the child would prefer not to face – the playground bully can be releasing a wide range of frustrations that he or she cannot consciously face

- projection – placing one's faults some distance away from oneself. This occurs when an individual sees unliked aspects of himself or herself in others – children who seem not to get on can be similar to each other

- repression – allowing anxiety-inducing events to be forgotten. This protects the child from having to take any decisions relating to the event, and from facing the anxiety associated with it. A repressed child is likely to be passive and obedient

- intellectualisation – avoiding the pain of feelings by thinking through one's emotions rather than experiencing them for what they are; for example, a boy left out of the football team avoids crying by talking only about the skills he needs to develop

- denial – when an experience is avoided rather than experienced. This can be seen, for example, in the child who will no longer talk about a very special friend who has moved away from the area

- reaction formation – the turning of a negative emotion on its head. An unacceptable impulse is mastered by an exaggerated expression of its opposite. A child who is obsessively tidy and organised, for example, could be masking a desire to let go and be messy.

It is worth restating that boys tend to use different defence mechanisms from girls. Although this is not always the case, it is usual for boys to employ the first four in the list: compensation, regression, displacement and projection. These are defensive reactions and fit in with the idea of the biologically programmed 'fight' response. This can explain why boys seem to be more disruptive – they 'act out' their internal emotional conflicts and, as a result, get labelled as being troublesome to manage in class.

For girls the last four defence mechanisms in the list are more commonly used: intellectualisation, repression, denial and reaction formation. Girls are more prone to withdrawal, anxiety and depression. Their defences reflect the biologically programmed 'flight' response.

Once any of these defences are employed and become functional in protecting the child from inner emotional conflict, they are reinforced. The negative tension a child has about his or her inability to spell, for example, is contained when he uses denial as a defence. Winston, for example, claims that he is not particularly bothered about his poor spelling, although Swarupa is. The reduction in tension caused by this suppression reinforces the use of this defence mechanism, thereby making it more likely to be used again. What this can mean is that, for some children, the original need for these defence mechanisms has long passed but, because they were quickly over-learned survival responses, they are now hard to break. Even when the child has learned to spell he or she uses the same way of releasing negative tension out of habit. Just as we take the same path through a field, so children come to rely on the same tracks that seem to 'work' for them.

If we are able to discern which defence mechanism a child is using, we can move towards putting in place interventions that will assist him or her in finding more adaptive ways of coping with his or her emotional needs. This will enable the child to deal with the reality he or she is facing.

Features of each defence mechanism

1 *Compensation* – the underlying need for these children is to be recognised, admired and praised for their successes to conceal their shortcomings.

2   *Regression* – there is a strong need to act out all impulses.

3   *Intellectualisation* – there is a need to feel in control in all relationships.

4   *Displacement* – there is a need to find a scapegoat who will absorb hostility.

5   *Reaction formation* – the student needs to feel approval for good behaviour.

6   *Projection* – the student needs to find imperfections in other people.

7   *Denial* – there is a need to avoid conflict in social relationships.

8   *Repression* – the student needs to avoid intimacy.

The questionnaire and score table (Figures 3.2a and 3.2b) can assist in deciding which of the defence mechanisms is being used by a child.

Defence mechanisms are unconscious and rigid ways of coping with internal negative pressure. To help children we need to provide them with conscious methods of solving their difficulties. Having a profile of a child's preferred unconscious ways of coping enables us to work constructively to help him or her to relate to the real world.

Having identified a student's defence style we are now able to work with him or her to promote more adaptive coping styles through which he or she will relate to the real world in a more realistic manner. Defence mechanisms are maladaptive solutions that emerge from the unconscious and, because the unconscious is not directly linked to the outside world, they tend to distort the world.

Intervention techniques

The table (on page 71) is an *aide mémoire* as to the general type of intervention appropriate for each defence mechanism. The learner who over-relies on compensation, for example, needs to be taught new skills.

We can now understand why some children – influenced by their biology, gender, cultural myths and socialisation – develop maladaptive ways of coping with conflicts. These maladaptive ways of coping can become rigid and lay the foundation for more severe problems in adult life.

Why don't most children become severely disturbed adults? The answer to this is to be found in the next chapter.

SCORE CARD FOR DEFENCE MECHANISMS (each description scores between 1 and 5)

1 Compensation	SOMETIMES		RARELY		NEVER	
• need to be popular with peers	1	2	3	4	5	
• enjoy being the centre of attention	1	2	3	4	5	
• try harder than others to please	1	2	3	4	5	
• seek constant approval for work done	1	2	3	4	5	
• over-indulge any personal success	1	2	3	4	5	**SCORE......**

2 Regression	SOMETIMES		RARELY		NEVER	
• act impulsively	1	2	3	4	5	
• cry when unable to cope	1	2	3	4	5	
• lose his/her temper quickly	1	2	3	4	5	
• run away from difficulties	1	2	3	4	5	
• respond aggressively to challenges	1	2	3	4	5	**SCORE......**

3 Intellectualisation	SOMETIMES		RARELY		NEVER	
• try to solve problems and difficulties rationally	1	2	3	4	5	
• show difficulties in expressing his/her emotions	1	2	3	4	5	
• need to lead others	1	2	3	4	5	
• prefer to express ideas rather than feelings	1	2	3	4	5	**SCORE......**

4 Displacement	SOMETIMES		RARELY		NEVER	
• pick on weaker class members	1	2	3	4	5	
• feel angry at people who boss others	1	2	3	4	5	
• intensely dislike people who show off	1	2	3	4	5	
• find most peer relationships difficult	1	2	3	4	5	
• often become involved in petty disputes	1	2	3	4	5	**SCORE......**

5 Reaction formation	SOMETIMES		RARELY		NEVER	
• be very hard on peers who break rules	1	2	3	4	5	
• like rules to be black and white	1	2	3	4	5	
• set high expectations for self and others	1	2	3	4	5	
• have little tolerance for people with different standards	1	2	3	4	5	
• make sure that others know of his/her successes	1	2	3	4	5	**SCORE......**

6 Projection	SOMETIMES		RARELY		NEVER	
• dislike people who get their own way unfairly	1	2	3	4	5	
• feel irritated by people who cannot be trusted	1	2	3	4	5	
• hate insincere people	1	2	3	4	5	
• make a big thing of other people's weaknesses	1	2	3	4	5	
• become over-defensive about personal errors	1	2	3	4	5	**SCORE......**

7 Denial	SOMETIMES		RARELY		NEVER	
• consciously hide any personal weaknesses	1	2	3	4	5	
• do whatever it takes to make a good impression	1	2	3	4	5	
• withdraw and sulk when he/she fails to get his/her own way	1	2	3	4	5	
• have an optimistic disposition	1	2	3	4	5	
• avoid confrontations at all costs	1	2	3	4	5	**SCORE......**

8 Repression	SOMETIMES		RARELY		NEVER	
• show feelings very rarely	1	2	3	4	5	
• appear unaffected by other people's distress	1	2	3	4	5	
• do not like talking about unhappy events	1	2	3	4	5	
• do not readily engage in confrontations	1	2	3	4	5	
• find helping others difficult	1	2	3	4	5	**SCORE......**

Now place score in table (Figure 3.2b).

FIGURE 3.2A Defence mechanism questionnaire

69

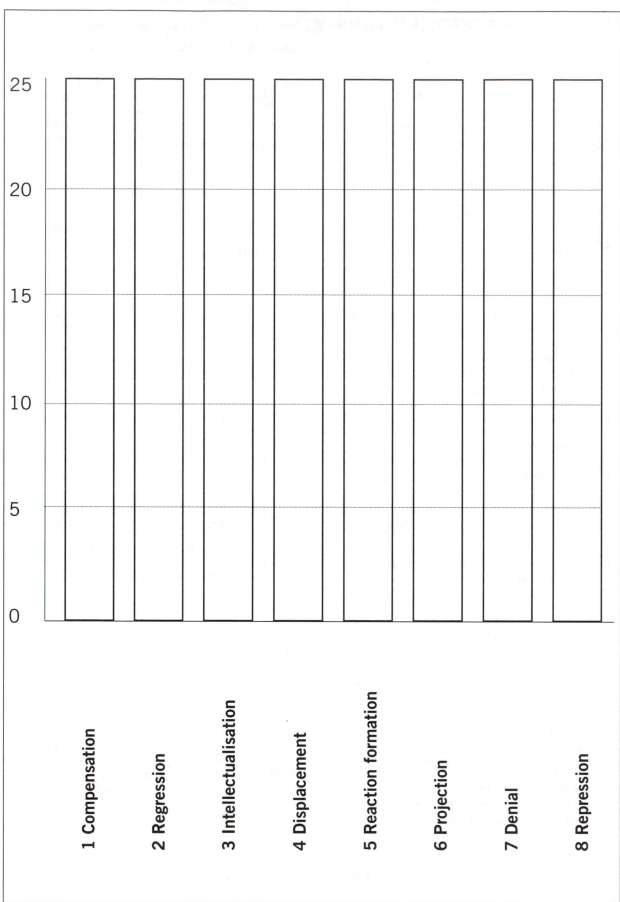

FIGURE 3.2B Score table for defence mechanism questionnaire

Defence coping style (unconscious and maladaptive)	Intervention (conscious and adaptive)
COMPENSATION	IMPROVE SHORTCOMINGS learn new skills
REGRESSION	HELP-SEEKING ask for help
INTELLECTUALISATION	MAPPING obtain more information on problem
DISPLACEMENT	SUBSTITUTION do unrelated activities to reduce tension
REACTION FORMATION	REVERSAL do opposite – put on a happy face
PROJECTION	BLAMING identify and blame causes
DENIAL	MINIMISATION reframe the problem
REPRESSION	AVOIDANCE avoid the situation or person

Adaptive coping styles

Figure 3.3 ties the different elements of our model together and, importantly, adds a key missing piece – adaptive ways of coping.

Defence mechanisms aim to avoid, distort or modify some perceived threat and, because they are unconsciously controlled, they are rigid and of limited value. Coping styles, by contrast, are conscious and can be used to replace the defence mechanisms. Coping strategies mean that painful realities are confronted and dealt with. Life is not pain-free and young people experience fears and rejections as we all do, but through facing them they do not hold negative emotions within themselves.

The interventions detailed here are in fact problem-solving techniques. The reason most children do not become disturbed adults is that they employ adaptive coping styles. The earlier we can build these into either a reactive programme to help an individual student or, better still, into a personal, social and health education (PSHE) curriculum, the more effective we will be. In a way the ideal situation is to adopt a 'psychological immunisation' programme – we need to promote healthy problem-solving techniques for *all* students.

Mapping

This process involves obtaining more information before tackling a problem or a perceived problem. If a student is upset because he or she has not been asked to a party, for example, he or she should find out why by asking someone. Was it a careless mistake? In this way the student can avoid jumping prematurely to unwarranted conclusions.

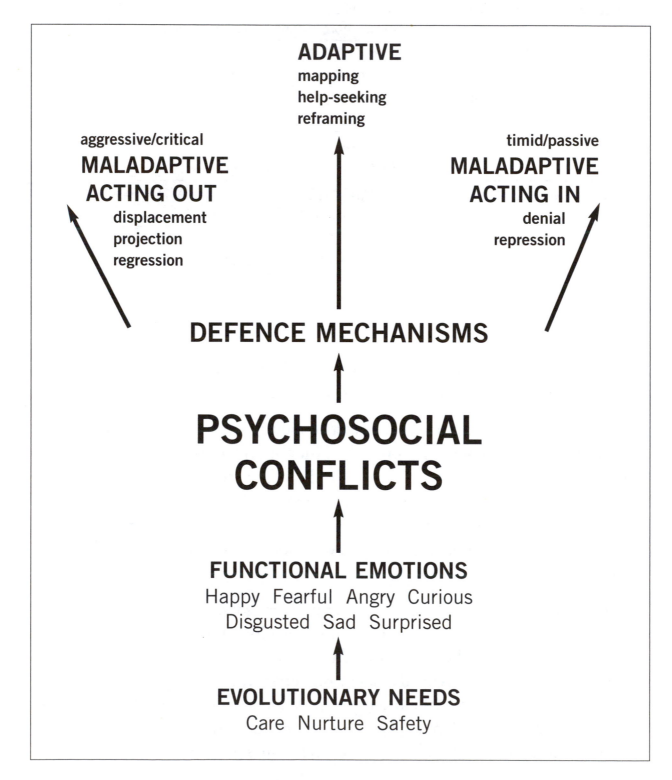

FIGURE 3.3 Emotional developmental model with adaptive coping styles

Intellectualisation as a defence mechanism occurs when decisions are made with very little factual evidence. Gathering information does not remove a problem – if the student was deliberately not invited to the party, then there is a problem in the 'friends' that our student has. Mapping is a conscious attempt to understand the world, whereas intellectualisation is a process that seeks to avoid the painful reality. If a student fails a test, he or she could intellectualise that it was the teacher's fault. But if he or she mapped the situation the student might see that not enough effort was put into preparation for the exam.

Avoiding

If the cause of a problem can be identified then a technique we all use is to avoid the person/situation. If a student has major relationship difficulties with a peer or tutor then reallocation can be a rational move. The degree to which this can be achieved might sometimes be small depending on the amount of control the student has. If the situation is unavoidable then the student would need to seek help and support from his or her tutor.

(Taken to extremes this technique can have a high price. A fear of flying can restrict opportunities to visit other countries. A fear of maths, developed in the classroom, means that a student might avoid any subject that involves numbers, with the consequence that many career opportunities are excluded.)

When a student uses repression, he or she pushes the difficult situation out of his or her consciousness, which can result in the student often being timid and passive in an attempt to forget painful events. Avoidance, however, faces and acknowledges the reality of the situation.

Help-seeking

For most students a key technique is to ask friends for help. The world is a much friendlier place if you have one person on your side. Isolated students can, of course, be more vulnerable without this support. It is vital, in giving these students the confidence to seek help, to build a relationship with them so that they feel safe and valued. Help-seeking means exploring ideas and solutions with people you know and trust. At times the friend may be a professional – doctor, nurse, teacher or counsellor.

The defence mechanism of regression is a commonly observed event in many classrooms. When faced with challenges that cause anxiety the child returns to earlier ways of responding, with immature behaviours such as hiding under tables, crying or running away. Help-seeking is a way of gaining support that is needed. There are many challenges that children face that they cannot resolve for themselves – bullying being one example – where they need adult or more expert support.

Minimising

Students can 'awfulise' problems out of all proportion to their importance. Being very close to an issue can negatively affect a person's ability to judge it. Minimising involves reassessing the importance of a problem. For example, a student who expected to be top in a test can react very negatively because he or she has exaggerated the importance of the test and is at risk of using denial as a way of coping and not responding to the reality. Minimising allows the student to ask such questions as: 'Will it be a problem five years from now?', 'Ten years from now?', 'Is this a real problem or an inconvenience?' Minimising does not mean that the problem is denied, but it is looked at in a different perspective.

Using minimising as an intervention in place of the maladaptive practice of denial means that instead of learners seeing problems or difficulties as being of no consequence, as they do in denial, they deal with the challenges they are faced with by reframing them.

Reversal

To cope with many situations we all learn to display the opposite emotions to those that we are actually feeling. This is not hypocritical but a positive way of coping. For example, we might sit calmly in the dentist's waiting room when we feel the opposite of calm. Similarly, students might show courage and calmness while rock climbing when in fact they are feeling quite scared. To display our true feelings all the time would not be helpful. Being scared when speaking in public will not enhance our performance, but through turning the nervous energy on its head we can act confidently and succeed. Similarly, if we are in a confrontational relationship with an adult or peer, then our verbal and non-verbal messages will be confrontational. However, if we act more positively towards them we can start to build a better relationship.

Reversal is a conscious attempt to use the negative emotional tension that we have to good effect. It can help us to accept that we have wishes and desires that we would prefer not to have, but we are able to accept the darker side of our nature and keep such impulses in check though conscious control rather than the maladaptive practice of reaction formation.

Blaming

This is not a long-term solution to problems, but there are times when we can help ourselves feel better by laying the blame either on situational factors or other people, when what has happened is indeed not our fault. There are times when problems are caused by factors outside ourselves, and to blame ourselves would be inappropriate, such as when accused of not having the right equipment when in fact someone has stolen ours or when told not to shout out in class when in reality it was someone else.

The maladaptive practice of projection leads to faults being found in others that are not based in reality. Blaming is a conscious appraisal of the situation, and causes are laid at the feet of those who are truly responsible.

Substitution

Sometimes students cannot escape situations they do not like; for example, being hit by a hockey ball on a muddy playing field in January or having to work with peers they do not really get on with. However, they can develop alternative areas of interest to compensate for this: joining the choir instead of shouting out loud; doing judo or karate to allow aggressive feelings to be worked through safely.

The maladaptive practice of displacement leads individuals to attack other people as a way of relieving negative feelings that cannot be expressed. Substitution allows the relief of such negative feelings in areas where there is no harm to others.

Improving shortcomings

There will be times when a problem is worsened through the student lacking certain skills, which could be organisational skills or self-control. If a learner lacks the ability to organise their work appropriately, they may compensate by being boastful about their ability to take on additional work and responsibilities to prove that they can cope. This only worsens the situation and leads to problems in many aspects of their school life. Acknowledging their weaknesses and seeking to improve skills by breaking tasks down into small but achievable targets enables the student to change their negative impact.

Multiple coping strategies

As adults employing these coping methods successfully we do not use any single one in isolation. To be adaptive we all use a number of them together. For example, if we are not very good at managing our money we may look at those areas of our lives that seem most difficult (mapping); arrange to meet with our bank manager (help-seeking); and take up evening classes to enable us to apply for better-paid work (improving shortcomings). This flexibility is important and students can be helped to choose a range of adaptive coping strategies to tackle the challenges they will inevitably face in their lives.

Multiple coping strategies in action

Adela is extremely unhappy in school. One group of girls seems to be systematically making her life unpleasant. They call her names, pass notes with untruths about her around the class and seem to be encouraging other girls not to play with her. In order to cope with this situation Adela plans to talk with her tutor (seek expert help); join a lunchtime drama group (improve shortcomings); and keep an accurate account of what is happening (blaming).

Conclusion

We have explored how early childhood tags can become more of a hindrance to learners than a help. We have also seen how children naturally seek to avoid emotional pain, but that this can lead to an over-reliance on defence mechanisms. Because the early years are so influential in the pathways that children take towards adulthood, schools need to have an awareness of the positive ways in which they can support all children. Ian is an example of a learner who, with support, turned away from becoming an adult who feared failure and was unable to engage successfully with others (see p. 77).

Ian

Ian was one of four children in a family that had experienced hard times through both parents being made redundant. His parents were critical of each other, and this seemed to pervade the children's relationships as well. Ian had communication difficulties that were resolved through intensive speech therapy. The combined effect of these factors was that Ian had learned to cope through being restless and disruptive in class (regression). His relationships with other children were characterised by his being bossy and taking charge of the games he played (compensation). When watched in the playhouse it become obvious that he would often bully one child until she cried (displacement). When challenged and punished because of his behaviour he would blame other children for provoking him (projection). He avoided any new learning task; at such times he could not be encouraged to try even the smallest task (fear of failure).

These behaviours led to Ian being labelled as experiencing SEBD, although this generic label helps neither Ian nor his class teacher. It is merely a description of his difficulties – not an explanation of them or a solution.

Through using the models suggested in this chapter, however, the class teacher was able to develop a programme that enabled Ian to learn new coping skills. The programme involved:

- allowing Ian time to engage in energetic sporting activities – football and running
- finding an area of natural interest to Ian – trains – and then developing reading and number skills using train-related activities
- teaching Ian self-control by showing him the consequences of his behaviours
- practising alternative behaviours to use when frustrated, such as going to a quiet corner to read a favourite book
- developing Ian's social skills by letting him work for short periods of time with a peer, and then allowing each child to choose a favourite activity.

Such interventions did not change Ian immediately, but over a period of six months the improvements were noticeable. Ian had more confidence, played happily with his peers and would willingly engage with learning.

Further reading

Reference

Plutchik, R. (2000) *Emotions in the Practice of Psychotherapy*. Washington: American Psychological Association.

Recommended reading

Denham, S. (1998) *Emotional Development in Young Children*. London: The Guilford Press.

Herbert, M. (2003) *Typical and Atypical Development*. Oxford: BPS Blackwell.

Lewis, M. and Wolan Sullivan, M. (1996) *Emotional Development in Atypical Children*. New Jersey: Lawrence Erlbaum Associates.

Lieberman, A. (1993) *The Emotional Life of the Toddler*. New York: Free Press.

Rycroft, R. (1972) *A Critical Dictionary of Psychoanalysis*. Aylesbury: Penguin Books.

# Yeah Right! Adolescents in the Classroom

Introduction

Knowing how to drive a car is obviously important for any aspiring driver. But so also is having a map of the country you are going to drive in. The same applies to all who work with adolescents. Knowing how to listen and respond supportively is vital, but so also is knowing something about the nature of being an adolescent today.

For too many there can be an attitude of 'I was a teenager once, therefore I know what it is like.' This does not follow. When we each imagine our own childhood we are viewing it from our hopes, fears and values of today. Even if we had not lost the key to our own adolescence we cannot inhabit the world of today's teenagers. We all develop in a unique time and the issues are unique to that period. Pressures differ, fears differ. The value of education changes over time as well. There are times when education is seen as the key to work opportunities, and others when it is not. There are times when school staff are highly valued. And there are times when schools are seen to be part of the problem rather than the solution.

Is there more disruptive behaviour in schools today?
The simple answer to this often-asked question is probably 'Yes'. But the reasons lie more outside teenagers than inside.

How schools have changed

For some young people the way we teach today can be difficult for them. In the past we had a passive view of learning. Children entered schools as empty vessels and our task was to fill them with knowledge. They sat in rows in front of an expert. When we needed to understand how they learned we turned to Piaget – for within child explanations. When we wished to control their behaviour more effectively we looked to the work of the behaviourists – who helped us to use the 'carrot and stick' more effectively. Today matters have changed considerably.

Now we have an active model of learning which involves young people much more. We look to the ideas of Vygotsky to help us understand the social nature of learning. We expect young people to work collaboratively in groups, to share, build on ideas, give critical feedback, etc. There are many children who lack the necessary skills to work in this way and they often mask this inability through 'acting out'.

How society has changed

Other major changes include the very way in which our society has changed. In the past there were many powerful institutions socialising children to behave 'appropriately'. These included:

- family
- community
- church
- schools.

Our work in school was reinforced by children's involvement with these other social agencies. Today for many children the church has little or no influence. Communities are much more fragmented, without an established and coherent identity. For many children the family itself has broken down, with the result that children experience conflict and pain.

The school is the one social context for many children that sets boundaries, adheres to core values and sets consequences when behaviour falls outside what is considered acceptable. For some children school is the only place where they are expected to conform to such standards. They are used to walking away from those situations that they do not like, so it is little surprise that schools are where we see many children 'acting out'. It is a reflection of the times we are living in.

The bridge to adulthood

Adolescence is a time when a child crosses the bridge to adulthood. To many adults it is seen as an unnecessary and tiresome period – the faster they can be pushed through it, the better. This view misses the nature and function of adolescence as a period of growth and development.

It is a period when boys challenge the authority figures in their lives. Because control is so important to boys they can find it difficult to acquiesce to the demands of adults. Their defiant behaviour – seen as a threat by adults – is their way of exercising their growing sense of adulthood. A typical scene is when the teacher politely asks the student to give him or her whatever it is the student is playing with. The student's denial and refusal to co-operate quickly escalates an innocuous request into a full-scale argument, with the student becoming agitated and angry.

It is also not uncommon for adolescent girls to have major disagreements with their mothers. Their negative and hostile behaviour in fact reflects their negative feelings towards themselves. As a girl moves towards womanhood she identifies with a significant role model. Her inside world is changing, she is becoming sexually mature, her body is changing – and not always towards the culturally held idea of beauty. She wants, subconsciously, to be like her mother and her frustration at herself comes out as aggression. In truth there is probably a large amount of envy. Understanding this does not remove the pain a mother can feel at the language her adolescent daughter uses to describe Mum; but it makes sense and can help her not to over-personalise every issue. In two or three years the same mother and daughter will be out shopping together and having fun.

Aims of this chapter

- to explore some of the developmental pathways adolescents take – for better or worse
- to detail two of the fundamental needs of adolescents:
  - who am I – identity
  - my way – personal autonomy
- to investigate the nature and function of 'risk taking'
- to present practical ideas to maintain and develop adolescent self-esteem.

Why 'Yeah right!'?

It is possible in our language to make two negatives a positive: 'I didn't do nothing' means 'I did something'. But making two positives mean a negative is no easy task. However this is exactly what is intended when an adolescent replies, 'Yeah right.' He or she means 'No'. Because we do not always understand the finer psychological nuances of adolescent communication, there are often misunderstandings and confrontations.

Another example of this faulty communication is when I ask my son, 'Can you please help me move some boxes?' I do not say it, but I mean 'now'. When my son answers 'Yes' he means he will help – but 'later'. We now have the perfect ingredients for an argument. Believe me!

And finally – arousal!

Before beginning to consider the three core aspects of identity, autonomy and self-esteem it is worth highlighting the nature and role of arousal in an adolescent's school life. The importance of hormones goes without saying – but there is another dimension to arousal that is often overlooked – the environment. The classroom can affect adolescents either positively or negatively. Briefly put, there is a part of our nervous system that responds to cues in the environment in an automatic manner: this is the autonomic nervous system. One part of this controls the 'fight or flight' response to arousal, which is part of our biological inheritance and is outside our control. Certain cues in the environment increase our arousal level: our heart rate increases and adrenaline is pumped into our bloodstream. For a short time such arousal can be positive, but if it persists it becomes distressing.

If we imagine negative arousal to be measured in a stress bucket (see Figure 4.1) we can see that, while we may differ as to how much stress we can cope with, there comes a level when it is unmanageable and it affects our thoughts, feelings and behaviour. An excessively hot or cold classroom will cause a degree of arousal in all adolescents. This may be manageable for most, but may contribute to one student becoming rude and quick-tempered. The temperature does not cause the behaviour – but it is a contributory factor.

Any environmental factor that increases a student's level of arousal, albeit not consciously noticed, will have a detrimental effect on performance, especially of complex tasks, if it is prolonged over a period of time. What is happening is that the student is having to divert energy in an attempt to reduce the external discomfort, leaving less to process incoming information.

Environmental stressors

Noise

Children working near to traffic noise were shown to make slower progress in reading and to have poorer hearing discrimination (Cohen *et al.*, 1973, quoted in Oliver, 2002).

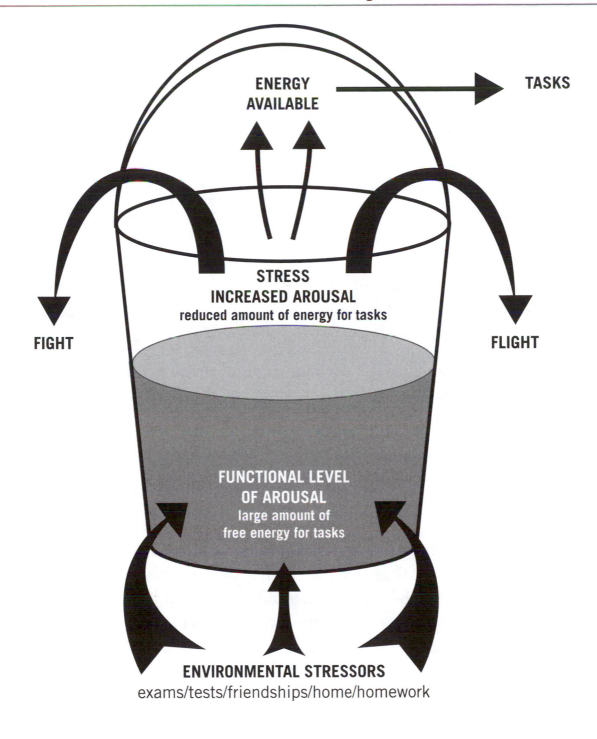

ENERGY AVAILABLE

TASKS

STRESS INCREASED AROUSAL
reduced amount of energy for tasks

FIGHT

FLIGHT

FUNCTIONAL LEVEL OF AROUSAL
large amount of free energy for tasks

ENVIRONMENTAL STRESSORS
exams/tests/friendships/home/homework

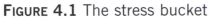

FIGURE 4.1 The stress bucket

Heat

Temperatures above 32 degrees centigrade negatively affect mental performance after two hours' exposure (Bell *et al.*, 1996, quoted in Oliver, 2002). Poulton (1970) found that temperatures below 13 degrees centigrade affected tactile discrimination and reaction times (quoted in Oliver, 2002).

Light

Research suggests that children perform better with natural daylight lamps rather than cool white fluorescent lamps. The suggestion is that cool white lamps cause higher arousal and distract children from learning (Munson and Ferguson, 1985, quoted in Oliver, 2002).

Territory

Young children are unaware of the rules controlling personal space. But by the age of ten, children are conscious of how close to stand to other people (Fry and Willis, 1971, quoted in Oliver, 2002). Overcrowding in classrooms and corridors results in young people having to invade each other's personal space. This invasion triggers increased physiological arousal in the invader and anger in the invaded.

This brief account highlights the need for environmental factors to be treated seriously, as they play a part in the reactions young people have towards their education and school staff.

Identity

Throughout childhood new skills and understanding are emerging. For key theorists each period of development has certain challenges that children need to pass through successfully. These are the building blocks for later development. If, for whatever reason, the child experiences difficulties then later development will be affected. The most popular theorist who has developed such a model is Erik Erikson. Figure 4.2 presents an overview of this model.

The early years are the foundation which enables a child to pass through adolescence successfully. It is during this adolescent period that young people:

- learn to think and reason abstractly
- mature physically and sexually.

During this phase there are many concerns that add pressure to their development. These include concerns about:

- education
- friendships
- sexual relationships
- leaving school – work.

DEVELOPMENTAL TASK	AGE	TASK	SUPPORT
Identity vs. Role	11–18	Identity	Acceptance/value Group, cause and exploration
Industry vs. Inferiority	6–11	Academic, social and practical skills	Develop skills
Initiative vs. Inferiority	3–6	Explore and be curious	Empower child, goals and projects
Autonomy vs. Shame and Doubt	1.5–3	Gain control	Give success 'Me do it'
Trust vs. Mistrust	0–1.5	Trust carers	Affection and consistency

FIGURE 4.2 Personal and social development

Adaptive development

The majority of children enter adolescence with a positive sense of identity. They have a sense of personal value and a realistic view of their skills. They have experienced successes and learned to cope with failures. They also have a balanced view of what is in their control and what is not.

During adolescence they will experiment with a range of 'possible selves'. Their music and dress will be expressions of their need for a sense of identity shared with others. Late adolescence sees them more clear about the kind of person they are, and able to make decisions about the kind of education or careers they wish to pursue.

Premature development

There are two types of premature development:

1 Foreclosure

For some children the range of choices that they have to make, the influences upon them and their desire to please so many result in 'foreclosure'. This is an early resolution of 'who to be'. But it is made before all the information has been considered or options explored. The adolescent is responding in a childlike way to the increasing pressures he or she either experiences or sees looming ahead. Such adolescents often decide on a career very early on and pursue it steadfastly.

2 Diffusion

A second form of premature development is when the child is just overwhelmed by all the alternatives and virtually 'gives in'. Such children become passive and dependent. They have given up the search for meaning to their lives and will pursue the path laid out for them by others.

Maladaptive development

The two pathways of premature development can lead to more extreme patterns of behaviour:

1 Acting out

Firstly, extreme foreclosure can result in adolescents following extreme role models. If, under pressure, they have developed challenging behaviour patterns then they may become delinquent in their behaviour and attitude towards school. School may be seen by them as the cause of all their problems. Their role may now be one of rebel within the classroom – this may well be reinforced by role models who are themselves anti-establishment.

2 Acting in

The second pathway leads on from diffusion. The nature of this young person's coping mechanisms is withdrawal and avoidance. Such responses are the breeding ground for depression, self-deprecation and a sense of worthlessness. Their behaviour in school is often that of the isolated young person; they have few friends and rarely participate actively. Their musical tastes can lean towards nihilism and a morbid attitude towards life in general and themselves in particular. Their self-care is poor, reflecting an inner sense of worthlessness.

Both these groups may turn to alcohol and drugs, but for different reasons.

For those who are 'acting out' it fuels their anger and rebelliousness. It shows to others their disrespect for the standards and expectations of people around them. The use of alcohol and drugs acts as 'macho' proof of their own power and indestructibility.

For the 'acting in' group it can be a way of escaping the stresses and pressures they feel, or it may at times lift their spirits and enable them to engage more successfully with their peers. Either way it becomes a form of self-medication to give meaning and encouragement in the face of extreme adversity.

The most extreme behaviours of each of these groups are seen in a small but significant number of adolescents who rush quickly into adult relationships or marriage. They seek reassurance through embracing what they see as adult solutions, under-age pregnancies, for example. Or, for the more negative and depressed group, whose extreme solution can be suicide – attempted or actual. This can be triggered when a 'hero' dies in tragic circumstances.

These different pathways are presented in Figure 4.3.

We can see that, while most adolescents have a dip into some form of foreclosure or diffusion, with support from peers and adults most return to the normal and healthy pathway through adolescence. We can all, however, name the few whose dip is more serious and enduring. Early recognition of such troubled young people can alert us to their needs and seek to ensure early support is offered in a range of ways to prevent the pathway becoming a permanent route.

It is of course important to note that schools and colleges are not therapeutic settings. Adolescents who show such problems as

● extreme withdrawal and isolation
● self-injurious behaviour
● suicidal intentions

ALWAYS need to be referred on to mental health colleagues.

However, for many adolescents school/college is a place where considerable support is received.

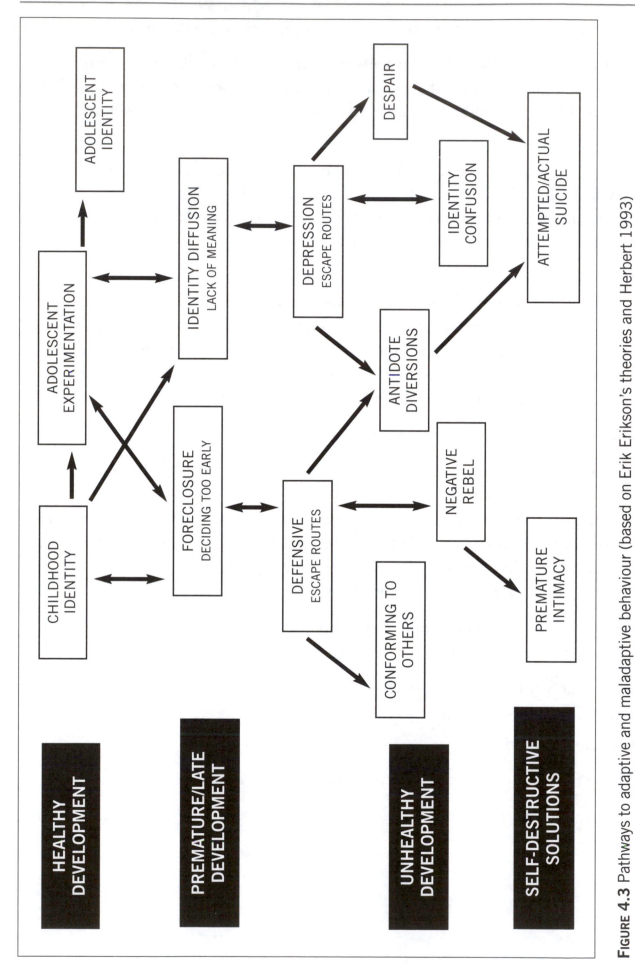

FIGURE 4.3 Pathways to adaptive and maladaptive behaviour (based on Erik Erikson's theories and Herbert 1993)

Support

Sexual identity

Adolescents will be coming to terms with their emerging sexuality. Information over and above that received in sex education lessons will be invaluable to those whose sexual identity is concerning them.

Relationship skills

For some adolescents immature ways of obtaining friends, and misplaced jealousy within friendships, can persist. Being disruptive in class may well have been reinforced by (negative) attention in the past, but during adolescence the student may well find peers are rejecting of him or her rather than amused. As a result there are some students who will benefit from social skills sessions. In such sessions they can learn and practise being part of a threesome relationship. They learn how to listen and enjoy listening, how not always to be the centre of attention, and how to cope positively with their feelings of jealousy which in the past would result in them acting out inappropriately.

Adolescent information

Good, clear and relevant information about the various changes that occur during adolescence will always be of value. The changes that are occurring physically as well as emotionally can be disturbing if they are not understood. Readily available information sheets, perhaps written by older students, can challenge the many myths that adolescents may believe – through such information what may seem abnormal can be normalised.

Coping mechanisms

To protect a weak self-esteem adolescents will develop a range of defence mechanisms. While this is normal, if they become over-dependent on them then problems can develop. During personal, social and health education (PSHE) lessons a curriculum could be presented which highlights positive ways of tackling issues that cause negative emotions. These range from learning new skills, through acquiring information to seeking adult help. The student who is being bullied, for example, could be helped by PSHE lessons in which a range of assertiveness skills are practised and by the teacher's assurance of students' rights to feel safe and protected in their school.

The 'macho culture' and 'saving face'

Adolescent identity is strongly influenced by identification with the peer group. In most instances this is, similarly, influenced by the fads and fashions of the music culture. This can in itself be a challenge in school regarding, for example, how much jewellery a girl should be allowed to wear. However there is a definite, and somewhat negative, set of subcultural values that has a much stronger impact in schools, and this is especially true in the case of boys.

It is the 'macho culture', the key aspects of which are:

- might is right
- size matters
- action not words.

In the past adolescents worked through these issues either outside school or in the playground. Today we see some young people bringing these issues into the classroom. The lack of respect held by many students for teachers and their status is a contributory factor to the increase in disruptive behaviour in classrooms. The reasons for these changes are complex but would include such changes as:

- the increased awareness of young people of their rights
- the reduced freedom of schools to choose the curriculum that suits particular students – this can be combined with a student's family not seeing the relevance of certain subjects
- the changing value of education as being relevant to work
- new teaching methods that allow students more freedom – this can result in a minority of students acting out frustrations.

In some schools adolescent boys are controlled by dominant teachers who are able to contain the disruptive behaviour because 'might is right' and they are bigger than the students. Teachers who try to instil such values as fairness, equity and democracy can struggle in such contexts.

The macho culture in school can lead to increased confrontations when adolescents are put into situations where they are likely to fail in front of their peers and consequently 'lose face'. There will be an increase in physiological arousal under such circumstances, which can result in a fight or flight response. Managing adolescents in such situations requires a sensitive balance between being target-oriented and providing sensitive support to prevent negative barriers being erected. Without this understanding many staff may ride roughshod over adolescents without appreciating that their own behaviour has, in fact, been part of the cause of the problem. School staff who use positive communication techniques to correct inappropriate behaviour are much more likely to be successful and less stressed than those who use overt confrontation techniques. For example, the teacher who demands that a student return to his or her seat and then stands challengingly to see that the student obeys is engaging in a win–lose contest – and there will always be the adolescent who will find losing an impossible option.

Alternatively, the teacher who states what is expected – 'You need to return to your seat and complete the work, thank you', and then turns away – is allowing the adolescent to choose to return to his or her seat. A win–win outcome for all concerned. (Real life is never as simple as this, but the techniques presented in the *Positive Communication* chapter in this book detail essential skills that can make a difference.)

Adolescents' identity is strongly influenced by the manner in which adults respond to them. They can learn to be critical not just of their own behaviour but of themselves. They can learn to feel ashamed rather than disappointed at their behaviour. Research suggests that people who feel ashamed of themselves are more likely to be aggressive towards others and less empathic (Tangney, 2002). Again, this reinforces the need for school staff to fully appreciate the importance of their communication style with adolescents.

Autonomy

Adolescence is a period where increasing autonomy is fundamental to moving towards adulthood. A key feature of adolescence is having increased control of such aspects as:

- friends
- interests
- values.

In the view of adolescents, being controlled by adults is what happens to children. They are no longer children, therefore many conflicts develop around adolescents wishing to make choices that the adults in their lives disagree with. But if we as adults are to respect the rights of adolescents to make choices, then we have to accept that there will be times when their choices are not in their best interests. We must remember that adults make mistakes as well – and they have the right to make those mistakes.

In the classroom the manner in which adults try to control adolescents' behaviour can be a 'red rag to a bull'. If adolescents conform to the adult's control, they are in danger not only of losing face with peers but also of failing to live up to their own expectations of being in control of their own behaviour. The manner and style that an adult uses in the school context will in part determine the reaction of the student.

A psychological definition of autonomy distinguishes between *reactive autonomy* and *reflective autonomy*:

- reactive autonomy is the tendency to act independently without being influenced by others
- reflective autonomy is to experience a feeling of choice about one's behaviour and its consequences for others.

In school it is reactive autonomy that causes so much difficulty. The adolescents who frequently confront school and classroom rules are those who have a strong need to act independently and find the constraint of rules and authority figures challenging. This kind of autonomy is 'act first, think second' – and the consequences of their impulsive behaviour can be negative towards both their peers and adults.

Developing increasing autonomy is a normal part of adolescence and is achieved through young people testing and pushing the boundaries that are placed around them. They do not know how free they are until they find the limits. While this naturally leads to confrontations within educational settings, they also experience fun in finding how free they are.

Why punishment does not always work

For a large number of adolescents who have trusting and caring relationships their move into increased autonomy is generally smooth. In school they accept the rules and find areas of interest where their increasing autonomy can be expressed. They have a strong desire to experience positive relationships with school staff and therefore work collaboratively with them.

However there are a sizeable number who challenge any school's authority to control them. These are the ones who are continuously involved with the school's discipline system. Every day students who fall foul of this system are short-term visitors. But there are others who are frequent visitors – the punishment system seems to make very little difference to their behaviour. Below are six key reasons why punishment systems fail, and will continue to fail:

1 Punishment/aggression cycle

Some students will perceive the punishment as being unfair, perhaps because there were mitigating circumstances that have not been taken into account, such as the teacher failing to notice that another student was provoking them which justified their response. As a result they feel hard done by and angry. Their anger leads to more aggressive behaviour; for example, they swear at the teacher for correcting them, and are then punished again. This vicious circle can quickly escalate and may result in exclusion. This all started from an adolescent's refusal to accept some minor correction.

2 'Fight' response

Whenever we are attacked the fight response is automatically triggered. Offence is the best form of defence and therefore some students will attack the punisher. This is especially true of students who have been punitively parented. Any challenge or frustration releases an over-learned aggressive response. This can be seen as the student becomes physically agitated, pushing desks and chairs, often as a prelude before he or she, usually, verbally assaults the adult involved. If cornered there is a real danger that the student will wildly hit out at any attempts to restrain him or her.

3 'Flight' response

Conversely, there is the flight response. If, for whatever reason, the adolescent is unable to attack the punisher then he or she is likely to run away to avoid the punishment. For example, when students see the punisher as more powerful than themselves, leaving the classroom is a way they can avoid escalating a conflict that they perceive as unwinnable.

4 Conditioned response

The person who gives the punishment can often become the object of a conditioned response. The emotional reactions of hostility and fear are triggered by the administrator of the punishment, which can result in the continuation of inappropriate behaviour. If it is always the same adult who does the punishing then his or her efforts to teach or befriend the student may be rejected.

5 Norm of reciprocity

Within all human groups there is a strong, unwritten rule, commonly expressed as 'You scratch my back and I'll scratch yours.' Basically it means that if someone does you a favour then you owe them one. Conversely, if someone hurts you, then you are sanctioned to pay back in kind – 'an eye for an eye'. The student who believes he or she has been unfairly treated by a teacher can feel justified in 'paying him or her back' by being rude, disruptive or uncooperative. There is a negative 'halo effect'. This means that whatever the adult does is seen by the student as being negative because of an earlier action. The student's negative feeling towards the adult colours the intentions he or she attributes to all of the teacher's future actions.

6 Disruptive behaviour works!

If the disruptive behaviour is functional for the adolescent – that is, it achieves certain benefits (escape from work, extra attention, for example) – then his or her negative behaviour is being maintained by a number of reinforcers. Simply introducing one negative consequence – the punishment – does not outweigh the factors supporting the behaviour.

There are, then, many good reasons why punishments with a certain group of adolescents are highly unlikely to succeed.

Developing positive reflective autonomy

Altruistic opportunities

Through giving students opportunities to help other students we are able to assist them in exploring the feelings that they have, as well as the feelings of the person helped. Disaffected students can learn much about themselves through supporting fellow students with profound and multiple difficulties; for example, by accompanying them on shopping trips, playing games or preparing meals together. This can help to develop and strengthen empathy. It may well be that the student has a limited emotional vocabulary and this will need extending. Teaching the student to recognise different emotions from different facial and bodily cues can be a useful starting point.

Self-monitoring

Developing a range of self-record schedules can enable students to take control of their behaviour. These can set specific targets that they wish to achieve – academic or behavioural. They could record the amount of work completed in set periods or monitor the number of times they leave their seat in a lesson. Through achievement students can be helped to attribute their improvements to the decisions that they have made and followed. For more detailed examples, see McNamara (1999).

Problem solving

Because many actions undertaken by students are made automatically with over-learned patterns of behaviour, such as always shouting out whenever they have a contribution to make, a problem-solving model will help. For example, work with the students to help them recognise why their behaviour is a problem; identify the different aspects of the problem (such as depriving others of a chance to answer); and plan alternatives to shouting out, such as writing down their response or sitting with and copying a role model. A commonly used plan is:

STOP... THINK... CHOOSE... GOOD CHOICE/BAD CHOICE

Many students will benefit from learning how to break problems down, explore possible solutions, weigh up the possible outcomes of different solutions and then decide which would be the most effective solution.

Risk taking

A characteristic of many adolescents who take up a lot of school staff time is their risk-taking behaviour. Such behaviour ranges from life-threatening, such as playing 'chicken' with traffic, to self-injurious behaviour through drug and alcohol abuse. As with most behaviour, there is no single, simple explanation for these activities. Awareness of the following factors can, however, help us understand why risk-taking behaviour in adolescents is not so weird and abnormal as it might first appear.

Stimulation seeking

Students vary in the degree of arousal they enjoy. Extraverts, for example, like a lot to be going on and when their nervous system lacks the degree of stimulation they need they will seek it out. Such students will find concentrating on one set task for any length of time difficult. School staff can help such students by providing them with relevant distractions, books and other activities.

Attachment theory

If a student experienced attachment difficulties as a child then these can resurface in his or her group behaviour. To be accepted by the group the individual will perform excessive acts, even violent ones, against non-group members in an attempt to belong to the group.

Group membership

If a group places a strong value on aggressive behaviour then new members can feel the need to show their commitment through exaggerating their behaviour to impress peers.

Group dynamics

Behaviours that an individual would not engage in on his or her own can become permissible within a group context. The individual may well believe that the fact that the group does not object to his or her behaviour means that they approve of it. Within relatively unstable groups there will be few established rules controlling behaviour, which can result in individuals acting out of character, as if the group were taking responsibility for their behaviour rather than the individuals themselves.

Immediate gratification

Adolescents tend to follow the law of effect – their behaviour is led more by the prospect of immediate consequences than long-term ones. Therefore the possible risk to themselves or others figures small against the immediate pleasurable outcome.

Immortality

As adolescents become aware of the finality of death, the fear that this can trigger can be avoided through a 'devil may care' attitude. Undertaking death-defying actions is their way of challenging their fear. Their survival shows that it is they who have the upper hand over this most human of fears.

While it is impossible to change the nature of adolescence we can try to channel and guide some of the natural propensities of young people going through this stage of development. Highly challenging sports can allow adolescents to learn to push themselves to the limits – but they must be undertaken with expert, professional guidance that both reduces the risks while teaching students the importance of preparation and skill training, etc. A group of students, for example, was rewarded for their co-operative behaviour with a potholing trip. The need for carefully supervised preparation enabled the students to appreciate the need to support each other as well as learning such skills as rope rock climbing.

Self-esteem

An area where adolescents can be vulnerable is in their sense of self-worth. There can be so many pressures from family, school, peers and the media as to how they should think, feel, behave and look that it is little wonder that many experience low self-esteem. It is often their attempts to protect their sense of worth that cause them to exhibit behaviour that brings them to the attention of school staff. They may act out in an aggressive and over-confident manner – the way they would like to be. But this is often a defence behind which lurks an adolescent with low self-esteem. This is unsurprising when you think of how the more at-risk group of adolescents have so little positive input: negative relationships with many adults, low academic self-esteem and sometimes poor peer relationships on account of their behavioural difficulties . . . anything that makes an adolescent stand out as being different can put him or her at risk of feeling inadequate and having low self-esteem.

Among the many factors contributing to low self-esteem, adolescents particularly at risk are those with:

- learning difficulties
- behavioural problems
- medical conditions
- physical and/or sensory difficulties
- early or delayed onset of puberty
- ethnic background
- social background.

While it is normal to feel low at times, there is a danger that during adolescence negative thoughts can be so over-rehearsed that they become automatic and over-controlling. Such an effect is more common during times of change, which is of course exactly what adolescents are going through. The ideas presented below are no quick-fix solution – that does not exist. Some of the ideas you are probably already using. Some will not be right for the student you are working with. Others might trigger a new idea that is just right.

The danger of low self-esteem is that it can so easily become self-perpetuating. Students with low self-esteem will select those negative events around them which can add to their gloom. It is as though they are in a hole, but they cannot stop digging and their gloom seems to demand more negativity to feed on. Vimla, for example, believes her essays are below the standard of her peers and that it is because she lacks ability. She does not see the point of trying hard when she will 'inevitably' fail, so she makes little effort and her failure increases.

Some ideas for enhancing self-esteem in 'at-risk' adolescents

- *Look for positive events for them to attend.* It can be so easy to stay in bed! Encourage them to attend films, plays or sporting events that interest them. This will give them something positive to discuss and distract them from negative thoughts.

- *Help them choose uplifting music to listen to.* Music is often an important aspect of young people's lives; however, they can become interested in music which is morbid and nihilistic. More uplifting music, maybe classical or jazz, can help them contribute to creating a more positive ambience.

- *Help them develop relaxation skills.* Low self-esteem can lead to worries and anxiety, which push the nervous system into overactivity. Learning to breathe properly and to unwind help to prevent the young person's nervous system becoming over-stressed.

- *Develop a daily exercise programme.* Exercise helps to release endorphins in the brain which will automatically make them feel better. Feeling good about their physical appearance is also a bonus at a time when that is so important. It is sensible, however, to avoid an excessive approach to fitness.

- *With the adolescent, develop achievable targets, record progress and celebrate.* If there is a project where the young person's skills are ahead of the adult – for example, in mechanical repairs – then this can increase his or her sense of competence. In addition, a common goal shared by adult and student gives the student an opportunity to experience an appropriate role model. Spending time with students also conveys a sense that you value them for who they are.

- *Understand the importance of their looks and physical appearance and support them as much as possible.* A school dress policy that allows older students to wear a limited amount of jewellery may be one way. Providing outside speakers who can talk informatively about fashion and creative dressing with a limited budget would be popular with most students.

- *Link them into challenges where they can receive genuine feedback.* Some young people who lack confidence will become inactive and withdraw from situations where their qualities and skills could be valued. Create opportunities for students to share any interests and knowledge that they have in areas that interest other students (for example, popular films, martial arts) by supporting them in giving short inputs to younger, less challenging students.

- *Avoid doing things for them.* It is important to develop and maintain a sense of personal competence. Sensitive support in a subject they find difficult allows students to explore ways forward for themselves, rather than entrapping the adult into solving the problem for them.

- *Support them in doing random acts of kindness each day.* Encourage them to support other students – for example, through a buddy system – or to develop links with community organisations such as the RSPCA. Helping others helps both the receiver and the giver.

- *Enlarge any school photographs of their successes or valued pieces of their own work.* This acts as a reminder of their real achievements.

- *Ask them to help you in some project.* Practise strategic incompetence, for example, 'Can you help me find this website?' Adolescents must find it depressing being surrounded by over-competent adults all the time – to be able to do something an adult can't can improve their self-esteem.

- *Make time to be with them for the pure pleasure of enjoying their company so that they know they are appreciated for themselves.* This might be a short chat at the end of the lesson about a common interest, such as sport.

- *A busy class teacher or assistant might also write a note to tell them he or she enjoyed their contribution in the lesson.* Such small gestures can convey to the student a sense of being valued.

- *Talk to them to help them to remember the many good things they do and have done.*

- . . . add as many more as you can think of.

Further reading

References

Erikson, E. (1965) *Childhood and Society*. Harmondsworth: Penguin.

Herbert, M. (1993) *Working with Children and the Children Act*. Powys, Wales: The British Psychological Society.

McNamara, E. (1999) *Positive Pupil Management and Motivation*. London: David Fulton.

Oliver, K. (2002) *Psychology in Practice – Environment*. London: Hodder and Stoughton.

Tangney, J. (2002) Constructive and destructive aspects of shame and guilt. In A. Bohart and D. Stipek, *Constructive and Destructive Behaviour*. London: American Psychological Association.

Recommended reading

Blum, P. (2001) *A Teacher's Guide to Anger Management*. London: Routledge Falmer.

Davie, R. and Galloway, D. (eds) (1996) *Listening to Children in Education*. London: David Fulton.

Evans, J. (1998) *Active Analytic Group Therapy for adolescents*. London: Jessica Kingsley Publishers.

Hill, J. and Maughan, B. (2001) *Conduct Disorders in Childhood and Adolescence*. Cambridge: Cambridge University Press.

Sommers-Flanagan, J. and Sommers-Flanagan, R. (1997) *Tough Kids, Cool Counselling*. Alexandria: American Counseling Association.

Motivation

Introduction

Anyone working with young people has an interest in what motivates them. Why do children think, feel and behave as they do? Motivation is at the heart of teaching learners of all ages and abilities. With a clearer understanding of motivation in school we are better able to understand and support those young people who find learning at best a chore and at worst something to be actively fought against. Yet, while many students are quickly labelled as 'demotivated', they can seem incredibly motivated – not to be motivated.

There are many questions that, on the surface, seem baffling and confusing:

- Why will students work hard in one lesson but not in another?
- Why will a reward work one day but not the next?
- Why will students say they understand when they don't?
- Why won't students work when they could easily succeed?

One of the problems with understanding motivation is that the finger of blame is nearly always pointed immediately at the student. We have become so used to believing young people to be responsible for their behaviour that we tend to ignore the context they are in. We would all agree, however, that some lessons can be boring and that some tasks can be beyond the ability of a student. We need to look at motivation as something that is influenced by:

- the characteristics of the individual
- the context the individual is in.

The wider our understanding of motivation the more effective our interventions will be. Motivation is not difficult to understand, as this booklet will show. It will provide insight and understanding as well as diagnostic tools and interventions to support those children who, in certain situations, when faced with certain tasks, presented by certain people, lack motivation.

With motivation:

- goals and objectives are more easily achieved
- lessons are enjoyed
- absences are reduced
- teams and individuals function more harmoniously and effectively.

A motivated student is one who arrives on time to lessons, has the correct equipment and seeks appropriate support to ensure success.

Without motivation:

- effort and persistence are reduced
- increased support and supervision become essential
- conflict and disharmony increase
- absenteeism increases.

A lack of motivation can explain why some students make little effort to learn and fail to complete assignments that are within their ability. Such students do not participate in lessons nor do they ask for support when they fail to understand.

Some motivation myths

Myth 1 – students who do not try in school are unmotivated
False. Students who fear failure can be highly motivated to protect their self-esteem.

Myth 2 – achievement is greatest when the grades students achieve are awarded on a competitive basis
False. Students who have a history of failure will give up quickly as they expect not to succeed.

Myth 3 – the bigger the reward, the harder students will try
False. Without an expectation of success rewards fail to motivate.

Personal awareness

Often the best way to make sense of the factors that affect our students is to look within ourselves. As you work through the questions below think of how they might apply to a student you know. (Some possible answers are on p. 105)

Question 1 – think of one thing that you are quite good at
In a few words – how did you become good at it?

Question 2 – think of a personal quality that you feel good about
In a few words – how do you know you can feel good about it? What evidence do you have?

Question 3 – think of one thing that you are not good at
In a few words – what went wrong?

Question 4 – think of something that you did learn successfully, but which at the time you did not want to learn
In a few words – can you explain what kept you at it?

From a very personal and practical point of view we now have a range of key factors affecting motivation that apply not only to us but also to our students.

Successful learning depends on:

- *wanting* – the more a goal relates to a student's personal interests and emotional needs the higher will be his/her motivation
- *doing* – opportunities to practise a new skill or understanding are essential for good learning
- *feedback* – constructive, positive feedback maintains motivation
- *understanding* – the more a new skill or understanding is linked into a student's existing framework the deeper and more meaningful the learning experience will be.

A definition

Some important points seem already to be emerging. One of the key observations, however, is that students' motivation can vary across situations and from time to time. Our definition needs to reflect the changing nature of motivation.

> Motivation is a state of readiness or eagerness to change, which may fluctuate from one time or situation to another. This state is one that can be influenced.
>
> (Miller and Rollnick, 1991)

Tips for lesson planning

Any lesson can be motivating or demotivating. It is worth detailing those aspects of a lesson that can increase a student's level of arousal, that is his/her motivation to learn.

Beginning a lesson
- Do students know the lesson objectives?
- Is their curiosity aroused?
- Is the work linked to their personal needs and goals?
- Are they aware of the skills they will master?
- Is there a range of activities to be completed?
- Is there an element of fun and surprise?

During a lesson
- Are there opportunities for practice?
- Can students obtain support quickly and effectively?
- Do students work collaboratively?
- Am I using a range of teaching methods?
- Can all students achieve extrinsic rewards?

Ending a lesson
- Is there a constructive review of the lesson?
- Are students aware of how the new knowledge/skills fit with their existing ones?
- Do students receive feedback for effort, competency, participation and achievement?
- Have the students experienced success through increasing their control?

When students fail to engage with lessons there may well be good reasons:

- Is the work set at an appropriate level?
- Does the student have the necessary skills for success? (Listening, organisational, etc.)
- Are there any physical (visual) or medical reasons why they cannot learn successfully?
- Are you aware of any changes in a student's home circumstances that could be emotionally distracting?

The student's perspective

- Are you aware of the student's values, needs and expectations?
- Are the learning outcomes challenging and relevant to the learner?
- Does the learner have the necessary skills?
- Are there plenty of opportunities for practice and success?
- Are the targets meaningful?
- Have you involved the student in setting the learning targets?
- Are you giving regular feedback and encouragement?

Personal awareness exercise: possible answers (from p. 102)

Question 1
Practice, determination, feedback, encouragement, enthusiasm.

Question 2
Feedback, other people, friends.

Question 3
Lack of practice, criticism, no interest.

Question 4
Long-term goal, reward, to show people I could do it, to please others, to avoid punishment, overcoming a challenge.

The learning process and personality

There are, of course, many factors that affect how well students learn. A useful model to hold in mind is that of the learning stages that students, and we ourselves, go through (see Figure 5.1). This model has especial relevance for those older students who become disenchanted with subjects they find boring. They also find it hard to relate positively to those adults whose management style is confrontational. Adolescents are less inclined passively to accept being treated as children but being expected to act like adults.

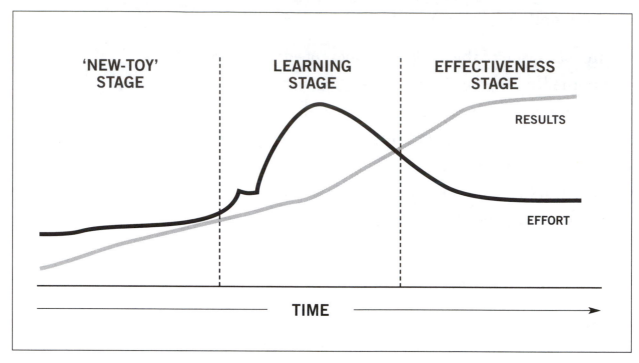

FIGURE 5.1 Learning stages

The motivational dip

It is common at the beginning of any enterprise, lesson, project, whatever, for there to be a high level of motivation/interest/arousal. *But* at the beginning of any learning there is a need for a lot of effort with very little payback as we try to master new skills or concepts. This scant return for maximum effort results in many students giving up. They experience what is known as the motivational dip (see Figure 5.2). (Who has not experienced this? It is normal.)

However if effort can be maintained through the early stages of an activity there comes a point when reduced effort produces increased returns as we master the task. Our aim for learners who are at risk of giving up quickly is to break tasks down into small achievable steps and to make sure that they receive feedback on their progress. At this stage the feedback needs to be specific and forceful to maintain their motivation through the motivational dip.

Recognition and feedback

Rather than being given rewards the learners need to be reassured that their efforts are paying off. We need to accentuate the positive when giving feedback on each of their small steps towards total success. Record sheets should magnify the progress they are making.

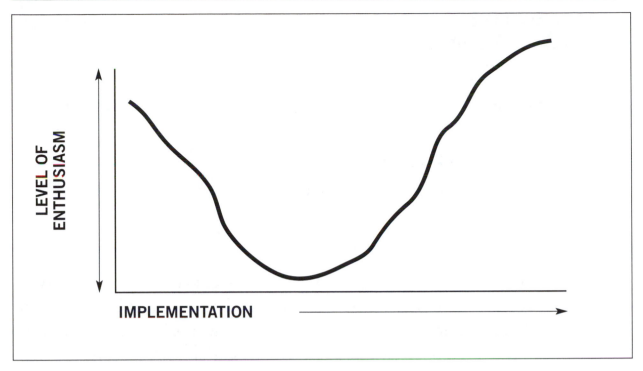

FIGURE 5.2 The motivational dip

Learning styles

Today we appreciate the different learning styles that students have. A well-known classification identifies three contrasting styles:

- visual
- auditory
- kinesthetic.

Individual learners prefer to receive new information in individual ways: either by seeing, hearing or feeling. While it is helpful to be aware of this, it is a rare lesson today where a teacher only uses one sense to input information to students. Most teachers tackle the differing ways in which students learn by using a range of methods in their lessons. For example a contemporary social topic is taught through showing Year 7 students video examples, letting them read actual accounts as well as interviewing participants of the events. Current topics could include investigating the need for skate parks or how young people's views are taken into account by local councils.

The best way to ensure that we vary our teaching methods is to remember the old Chinese adage:

I hear and I forget.

I see and I remember.

I do and I understand.

Another useful classification focuses on the preferred manner by which students process information. There are four common styles:

- *reflector* – likes to think and observe
- *pragmatist* – enjoys seeing how practical problems can be solved
- *theorist* – enjoys new ideas and concepts
- *activist* – enjoys hands-on experience.

Using this latter classification it is possible to see how certain teaching methods are likely to engage certain learning styles more than others. Figure 5.3 shows the most preferred methods for each learning style. It may be used as an *aide mémoire* to ensure that a lesson has a wide range of methods so that each student's preferred learning style is at times being tapped.

Personality style

If we compared the personality attributes of most school staff with those students who face social, emotional and behavioural difficulties we would see a marked contrast. School staff would probably score high on such attributes as being determined, hard working and committed, while our sample of students would score higher on rebelliousness, daydreaming and attention-seeking. We are not always in the best position to understand the challenges they face, but being aware of our students' different attributes enables us to try to ensure that some of the teaching methods we use tap into relevant aspects of their personality. Figure 5.4 shows that the rebel will enjoy role play, group work and real-life practice, while the dreamer will prefer problem-solving, reflection and observational learning.

By designing our lessons with reference to both these models we can ensure that they will enable as many of our students as possible to feel actively involved, using teaching methods that match their preferred thinking and personality style.

The learning profile

All students develop their own preferred ways of learning. This is the result of

METHOD	INFORMATION LEARNING STYLE			
	REFLECTIVE	PRAGMATIST	THEORIST	ACTIVE
ROLE PLAY				✓
REFLECTION	✓			
PROBLEM-SOLVING		✓		
GROUP WORK				
CASE STUDY		✓		
PRESENTATION			✓	
VIDEO	✓			
QUESTIONNAIRE			✓	
WORKPLACE PRACTICE				✓
QUIZ			✓	
OBSERVATIONAL LEARNING	✓			
PEER COACHING		✓		

FIGURE 5.3 Learning grid and methods

interactions between the individual (biology and developmental personal characteristics) and his/her social world. Knowledge of a student's learning style can help the student and us to construct preferential learning experiences that will engage and motivate him/her. It can also serve as a useful framework through which a positive relationship can develop between the learner and the adult.

Help the student complete the assessment profile below.

METHOD	PERSONAL STYLE		
	REBEL	DREAMER	ATTENTION SEEKER
ROLE PLAY	✓		
GROUP WORK	✓		
REAL LIFE PRACTICE	✓		
PEER COACHING			✓
1:1 SUPPORT			✓
SIMULATIONS			✓
PROBLEM-SOLVING		✓	
REFLECTION		✓	
OBSERVATIONAL LEARNING		✓	

FIGURE 5.4 Personal style and methods

Learning preferences assessment

1. Perceptual preference
Does the student prefer to listen, see or actively take part in new learning?

2. Learning style
What is the student's preferred learning style?

> activist
> theorist
> pragmatist
> reflector

3. Environmental factors

Does the student work better in the morning or afternoon? Does she or he prefer noise or quiet?

    noise v. quiet
    morning v. afternoon

4. Social factors

Can the student learn best alone or in the company of others?

The attribution process

Two core aspects of motivation are the student's self-worth and his or her attribution process. The attribution process is the way in which learners make sense to themselves of their behaviour. In other words, when learners fail, they might put it down to:

internal reasons
- they didn't revise enough
- they lack the necessary ability

external reasons
- they were poorly taught
- the questions were extremely hard – no one could do them.

Naturally the way they explain matters to themselves will affect their motivation in the future and their self-esteem. It is worth noting here that there is a general gender difference: girls tend to use more internal explanations when they fail – negative-prone failure attributions, while boys tend to use more external ones – they blame the teacher, the work, etc.

Student responses to failure

Why is it that two students who both fail a test respond so differently?

- Student A fails a test but becomes fired with increased determination to improve on the next one. The student knows that with more preparation he or she can make progress.

● Student B fails and becomes increasingly depressed. The student feels ashamed, and failure immobilises him or her, preventing preparation for the next test.

The difference between these students is the manner in which they explain their failure to themselves.

Attributional styles

Three common attributional styles that have been identified and studied are:

1. Learned helplessness

This is a lack of effort in specific situations. Through experiencing repeated failure learners come to believe that they are unable to succeed in certain tasks; that no matter how hard they try they will fail. Consequently they make little effort.

Such students respond to problems with a complete overreaction; failure seems to trigger a negative downhill spiral, a sense that they will never be able to improve, and results in such outcomes as 'maths phobia'.

2. Fear of failure

Learners who are prepared to attempt difficult tasks tend to attribute failure to internal causes, for example lack of effort. This means they are aware that they have some control and can therefore improve through effort. However, those learners who fear failure have a weaker self-esteem. They see failure as being caused by factors beyond their control and believe there is nothing they can do to improve their results. Fear of failure is an emotionally controlled way of protecting a learner's fragile self-esteem.

3. Lack of ability

Some learners are convinced that they lack ability and that no amount of effort can change this. When they do succeed they often attribute success to luck or easy challenges. 'Lack of ability' is the student's cognitive explanation for his or her failure.

By asking the right questions of the learner we can ascertain the type of attribution process she or he is employing in a particular situation. The right questions will also tap into three core aspects of the attribution process:

1. Locus of control

Does the student believe the reasons for failure are within his or her control (internal), or not (external)?

2. Stability

Is the student's success or failure a short-term occurrence or predictive of future outcomes?

3. Control

Does the student believe she or he can change matters or not?

Through circling the answers a student gives in Table 5.1 it is possible to see whether it is faulty attributions that are contributing to a student's lack of motivation.

Attribution training

It is understandable that attribution processes that have been learned over time are not going to be quickly changed. If learners have formed the mind-set that when they fail it is because of their lack of ability or the teacher's poor instruction, for example, a major change of perspective is required for them to believe that with more effort they could do better. It is comparable to turning the naturally pessimistic person into an optimist. It can be done – but it takes time. There are a number of techniques that can be used to help develop the learner's belief in his or her own power to overcome difficulties and the assurance that success is not impossible.

Effort training

Teach learners to recognise when their failure is due to low effort and reward them when they acknowledge this. For example, ask the student to gauge on an effort scale how much effort they think a particular task is going to take: 'So, Jack, to complete this page of maths problems how much effort do you think it will need? Remember that yesterday the page you thought would require little effort, I think you gave it a 2 rating, was not as easy as you expected.'

Effort scale

Little		Moderate		A lot
1	2	3	4	5

DIMENSIONS	ATTRIBUTIONS	
	TEST SUCCESS POSITIVE	TEST FAILURE NEGATIVE
INTERNAL V EXTERNAL	**LOCUS OF CONTROL**	
	I WORKED HARD	I DIDN'T REVISE
	I WAS LUCKY	BAD LUCK
STABLE V UNSTABLE	**STABILITY**	
	I'M GOOD AT TESTS	I GET STRESSED
	I WORKED ON THE RIGHT TOPICS	IT WAS A HARD TEST
CONTROLLABLE V UNCONTROLLABLE	**CONTROLLABILITY**	
	I PLANNED AND REVISED	I REVISED OTHER SUBJECTS TOO MUCH
	SOMEBODY UP THERE LIKES ME	WHY DOES EVERYTHING ALWAYS GO WRONG

TABLE 5.1 The attribution process

Success training

Set realistically obtainable goals. For example, 'OK, Shakeela, you are going to write a short story about your holiday. Let's look at what will be your first steps then we can build it from there. You were telling me about the people you were going to include. That sounds like a good place to start. Make a list of who is going to be in the story, and then describe them.' When learners succeed at their goals, support them in attributing their success to the effort they put in.

Cognitive dissonance

This is when two thoughts conflict with each other. Thinking negatively about sport and then volunteering to join a team activity produces a tension that needs to be resolved. In adults a common example would be 'I know I smoke', but, conversely, 'I also like to keep healthy'. With encouragement and advice on how to tackle areas of particular difficulty learners can be helped to succeed. The adult can then highlight the discrepancy in their thinking: 'You said you couldn't do that problem. But look, you have. You'll have to tell yourself you can do those problems from now on.'

Challenging

With a supportive adult the learner can examine some of his or her faulty beliefs against the evidence he or she is using. For example, 'You're saying you've had a really bad term. Let's have a look at your results because I am not sure they are as bad as you think.'

Reframing

The learner can be helped to explore a number of alternative explanations for his or her behaviour. For example, 'You are disappointed at your homework mark, but let's look at the pressures you have been coping with lately. You have just moved into a new house and you told me last week that your Gran was in hospital. Do you think these worries might explain why you have not been so focused on your work and why your mark was lower than usual?'

Self-reinforcement

The learner records and monitors his/her own behaviour over a period of time with agreed rewards for achieving set targets. For example, a student who leaves his or her seat for no sensible reason could record every time he or she does so. If the number is below a set target (perhaps six times in a lesson) the student can be allowed an agreed reward, such as extra computer time, to choose the class story book, etc.

Assessment tools and interventions

The causes behind an individual learner's behaviour comprise many interlocking factors, some of which are difficult to understand, and we may never have a complete picture of the complex set of influences in each student's life. Any attempt to explain behaviour is always, in any event, a gross simplification. Some of the factors to consider are:

- biological factors – such as an inherited disposition to be tall or short
- genetic factors – such as dyslexia
- developmental phase – what level of emotional self-control they have achieved
- family – for example, parenting style (authoritarian, authoritative, democratic)
- attitude – for example, 'you have no right to make me work at home'
- personality/temperament – are they calm or prone to anxiety?
- attributions – do they quickly blame others or accept responsibility for their own behaviour?
- school experiences – do they feel safe and part of their group?
- etc., etc.

But we are not looking for definitive explanations. We are looking for clues that help us understand the reason for a learner's behaviour in a particular context. This is much easier and more relevant to us when we are seeking appropriate interventions. Drawing on theoretical explanations as well as applied research we will look at two practical approaches to help us understand and support those students who do not engage with our lessons.

The first we will call *a functional analysis of behaviour*. This allows us to understand the 'why' of our students' behaviour through looking at what it achieves for them. Kate, for example, is frequently out of her seat and disrupting other students. As a result her teacher has to keep reprimanding her. A functional analysis of behaviour will ask what Kate's behaviour is 'earning' for her. It seems that there are several related needs being met:

- Kate is avoiding work
- Kate is receiving both peer and adult attention.

By understanding the function of her behaviour we can use interventions that will help Kate satisfy some of her needs in a less disruptive manner.

The second approach considers what we will call *motivational barriers*. By this I mean those commonly understood reasons why some students seem to lack motivation to work (see list of motivational barriers on pp. 117 to 120).

Many of the problems that demotivate and prevent students from engaging with the work they are set stem from what are known as *mistaken goals*:

- *habitual* – an over-learned pattern of behaviour that occurs automatically in specific situations – as seen in the student who argues whenever confronted with learning challenges

- *attention* – the need for attention, even if it involves negative feedback – from the student who seeks reassurance and approval after each small step is completed. In a Year 2 group, for example, Randeep is painting a picture of his house and garden. Every time he draws in a small part he leaves his seat to ask his teacher, 'Is this all right?' In 15 minutes he has left his seat eight times

- *power* – the need to have control in situations by challenging any reprimand and being prepared to increase the conflict

- *revenge* – the need to cause pain and hurt as a release to personal pain – demonstrated by the student who secretly spoils another child's painting, for example

- *nurture* – the need to have an adult who will care and parent them as, for example, when a student is unable to attempt work unless supported by an adult one-to-one

- *escape* – the need to avoid work that could lead to failure – shown by the student who engages in avoidance activities such as sharpening pencils.

Whether it is these mistaken goals that are driving a student's behaviour in class can be discerned through asking good questions. Because behaviour is functional, that is it seeks to obtain a certain outcome, we can often infer the mistaken goal that is driving the behaviour by looking at what it achieves for a student. Figure 5.5 presents a range of indicative questions that will enable us to hypothesise which are the strongest influences behind a set behaviour. It is not uncommon for behaviour to be driven by several factors – young people are as complicated as you or me.

Now that we have one or two hypotheses we can choose some interventions that we can use to help the learners satisfy their internal needs in ways that are more appropriate within the school and classroom context (see Figure 5.6).

Motivational barriers

Failure syndrome. Some students are so used to failing that they no longer make much effort. If you expect to fail, what is the point of expending excessive energy? These students are often able but have had negative learning experiences that have lowered their expectations.

HABITUAL

Does the behaviour:

1 Happen mainly when the student is on his/her own or bored?　　Y　N

2 Make the student unaware of his/her surroundings?　　Y　N

3 Stop when the student is distracted?　　Y　N

4 Have a set pattern/set of actions?　　Y　N

5 Persist despite requests to stop?　　Y　N

SCORE_____

ATTENTION

Does the behaviour:

1 Stop when attention is given?　　Y　N

2 Only happen when the student has an audience?　　Y　N

3 Start up when attention is withdrawn?　　Y　N

4 Lead to negative feedback?　　Y　N

5 Make you feel annoyed or irritated?　　Y　N

SCORE_____

REVENGE

Does the behaviour:

1 Take place in private?　　Y　N

2 Persist despite sanctions?　　Y　N

3 Seem to be aimed at one person?　　Y　N

4 Hurt either themselves or others?　　Y　N

5 Make you feel sad and despairing?　　Y　N

SCORE_____

POWER

Does the behaviour:

1 Happen repeatedly?　　Y　N

2 Lead to a confrontational response?　　Y　N

3 Make you feel angry or frightened?　　Y　N

4 Gain control for the student?　　Y　N

5 Escalate when confronted?　　Y　N

SCORE_____

NURTURE

Does the behaviour:

1 Make you feel sympathetic and caring?　　Y　N

2 Result in the student being cared for?　　Y　N

3 Start up again when support is withdrawn?　　Y　N

4 Seem aimed at the same person?　　Y　N

5 Only happen in social situations?　　Y　N

SCORE_____

ESCAPE

Does the behaviour:

1 Happen in response to work being set?　　Y　N

2 Stop when appropriate work is given?　　Y　N

3 Result in the student being withdrawn?　　Y　N

4 Take place in different lessons?　　Y　N

5 Take place with different adults?　　Y　N

SCORE_____

STUDENT'S NAME_____ COMPLETED BY_____

DATE_____

Figure 5.5 Motivational assessment – a functional approach

HABITUAL

1 Have distraction activities
2 Teach substitute activity
3 Reward timed sessions without behaviour
4 Use non-verbal signal to stop behaviour
5 Encourage small signs of improvement
6 Teach relaxation skills
7 Reward incompatible behaviour

ATTENTION-SEEKING

1 Reward appropriate behaviour
2 Catch them attending positively
3 Tactically ignore
4 Arrange regular 1:1 contact
5 Sit with peer who models appropriate behaviour
6 Use 'pay back' system for time wasted
7 Teach appropriate behaviour

REVENGE

1 Build self-esteem
2 Develop circle of friends
3 Make life map of successes
4 Explore feelings through creative mediums and Art Therapy
5 Agree 'reparation' activities
6 Agree safety boundaries
7 Develop empathy for others

POWER

1 Give responsibilities, school council
2 Side-step confrontations
3 Let them mentor a peer
4 Agree 'response plan' when confrontations develop
5 Let them lead an activity
6 Teach self-control
7 Give them choices

MURTURE

1 Reward 'I can' statements
2 Give safe choices
3 Strengthen and develop social skills
4 Teach positive self-statements
5 Highlight existing skills
6 Review challenges faced and overcome
7 Teach problem-solving skills

ESCAPE

1 Differentiate curriculum
2 Provide sensitive support
3 Agree small targets
4 Teach new skills
5 Reward requests for support
6 Use rewards for effort as well as achievements
7 Use peer support

FIGURE 5.6 Motivational assessment – interventions

Disaffection. It is not uncommon for some students, especially during the adolescent years, to become disaffected. This is a shorthand way both of saying they see little relevance to them of the curriculum they are expected to study and also of challenging the rights of adults to control them now that they are 'adults' themselves.

Underachievers. These students have a negative set of attitudes towards learning. They set unrealistic goals and yet tend to be too impulsive to persevere with assignments. These students often have the skills that would allow them to achieve, but see success as being dependent on factors outside of their control.

Boredom. These students tend to disrupt and distract others from their work. They convey an attitude of apathy and pointlessness towards any new activities. When they do work they expect rewards for the slightest effort they make.

Clearly, while these are listed as discrete motivational barriers, in reality most students will be affected by a mixture of several. An understanding of these different barriers does, however, allow us to become clearer as to the best interventions to put in place to support students who lack motivation (see Figures 5.5 and 5.6, pp. 118 and 119).

When we have produced a profile of some of the motivational barriers that a student is facing we can choose interventions most likely to prove effective from the intervention tool box.

Intervention tool box

Failure syndrome
- show faith and have positive expectations
- involve student in recording successes
- find a brilliant corner and harness it
- personalised differentiation – relate to learners' interests
- celebrate non-academic achievements
- make practice safe
- teach positive attributions for success

Disaffection
- build a relationship with the student
- let student set his/her own targets
- identify a role model
- arrange support for 'out of school' problems
- change the curriculum
- find a personal mentor they really like
- reward basics, e.g. attendance, punctuality, following rules

Underachievement
- differentiate and extend
- use alternative ways of learning
- get student to help someone less able
- explore reasons
- create a hierarchy of rewards
- encourage peer support
- set interesting homework and tasks

Boredom
- vary learning and teaching style
- make activities more exciting
- use games for learning
- give interactive/lively input
- encourage lively activity
- use music
- introduce sudden change of activity
- use discovery learning

The hard to reach

There will be a few children on whom the previous interventions will make little impact. These students are often described as being both reluctant and resistant learners. It is worth noting some of the negative factors that are probably holding a student in this state of affairs:

- a history of school failure
- negative adult feedback
- negative attitude
- poor organisational skills
- confrontational defence style
- real or imagined peer approval

... the list goes on.

Student resistance

Our efforts to help students who are firmly trapped in an anti-learning attitude will typically meet with resistance. The harder we push the harder they push back – this response is in itself a normal psychological reaction. Such students are naturally reluctant to step into the unknown by responding differently to challenges than in the negative way that they have learned over a long period of time. They are unlikely to change their responses just because you or I ask them to.

It is important to remember that, while we are attempting to change students' behaviour through positive interventions, there remain many negative factors in their life which support their existing behaviour. If ours were the only influences on them life would be so much easier! From the students' point of view their behaviour remains functional in fulfilling their needs and/or defending them from challenges that are beyond them.

Building a relationship with the student

It is relationships that give our lives meaning. Just think for a moment of the difference between an *interaction* and a *relationship*. Interactions are usually short in duration, functional and unemotional, while a relationship lasts for some time, is emotional and enjoyable.

Our approach in trying to reach such 'hard to reach' students is to create an open, honest and trusting relationship with the student. When we have that a student may begin openly to consider the advantages of change. Without such a relationship we are in danger of just being another 'well-meaning adult' trying to change them – and the student is understandably defensive. (Resistance to changing well-established patterns of behaviour is not abnormal – it is normal. All of us relapse when we try to break ingrained habits.)

Students with SEBD

Students with social, emotional and behavioural difficulties are at high risk of experiencing motivational difficulties. This is because their difficulties will usually have been barriers to them engaging with learning experiences. As a result they will tend to have had more negative experiences in school through reprimands and punishments and their attitude towards learning is not surprisingly negative, reflecting an apparent lack of motivation. In the learning situation they are likely to experience anxiety and insecurity.

The ways in which students react to such distress are likely to fall under two headings:

- *active defensiveness* – the student 'assaults' the authority figure by means of disruptive behaviour
- *passive withdrawal* – the student withdraws from the situation and will not contribute or respond when questioned. The student's fear of failure pushes him/her into a protective shell. Such students can easily be overlooked in a lesson because they present little active challenge.

These responses are more commonly known as 'fight or flight'. The challenge for any adult working with such students is to enable them to experience success as well as a sense of hope that matters can improve through a secure and trusting relationship. The adult serves then as a mediator between the student as learner and the task to be learned.

Note. The relationship we need to build with our students is, of course, a professional one – we are not looking to become their best friend and we need at all times to make this clear. If we are working with adolescents they can easily, and sometimes wilfully, misread our attempt to build a supportive relationship with them. If a relationship begins to make you feel uneasy, be guided by your emotions. Discuss the matter with colleagues. Try to work with the student only in small groups or when there are other adults present. Do not let matters get out of hand.

Relationship-building skills

General strategies

- spend time with the student
- disclose appropriate self-information, such as personal hobbies, football team supported, musical interests
- show high expectations
- develop rituals and traditions, for example play a special piece of music whenever a learner does something outstanding
- link with their friends and home.

Specific techniques

When you have built a positive relationship with the student you will be able to discuss and work with him or her to find ways to improve his or her motivation.

Cost–benefit analysis

Try to be clear as to the benefits students will obtain by improving their commitment to work. What are the advantages and disadvantages? Do they have a long-term goal? Does effort now play a part in achieving it? Help students to understand that it is not just 'the piece of paper' that they will achieve. They will learn a wide range of life skills:

- to work as a team member
- to be a leader
- to communicate
- to problem-solve
- to manage confrontations
- negotiation skills.

Norm of reciprocity

There is a fundamental norm at work in all relationships – it is known as the 'norm of reciprocity'. In English that means 'you scratch my back and I'll scratch yours'. If someone helps you or does you a good turn, then there is a degree of expectation/obligation that if they ask you for help you will help them. When possible the more help/support you offer students the more likely they are to help you when you ask. Offering to lend them books or equipment are all ways of investing in the 'emotional bank'.

Locus of control

Many students have experienced little age-appropriate autonomy and have little control in their lives. Refusing to work can be an attempt to gain some control. This will be especially true during adolescence – a time when they are expected to take more control over their lives. Some adolescents express their need for control by refusing to be helped by adults. Make every effort to allow them to set their own learning targets.

With the more difficult to reach students some of the following interventions may be used in conjunction with a good relationship:

Wagering

Students often like a challenge: 'I'll make you a coffee if you can complete this questionnaire in 10 minutes.'

Law of effect

Explaining what is in it for the young person if they make an effort to learn can help them to see what is to be gained or lost.

Personal notes

When a young person finds it difficult to talk, write them a note saying, for example, that you are glad they came and hope that they will talk when they are ready to.

Teaching strategic skills

Agree to help the young person achieve a specific goal and work with him or her to develop skills to achieve the goal.

Termination as motivation

'I understand that you don't want to have six sessions with me. How about it if we work hard and reduce that to three sessions.'

Cost–benefit analysis

Work out with students the gains to them of keeping with their present behaviour and the losses, and the gains and losses if they change.

Emotional change technique

Teach young people that by thinking of certain memories they can learn to change what they are feeling. For example, if they have an especially happy holiday memory, or a funny incident that happened in school, help them to use the memory to re-experience the feeling that they had. With practice they can change their mood by focusing on the memory and the feelings that went with it.

Scaling technique

On a scale of 1 to 10, with 1 being the worst this problem has ever been and 10 the best, where would you rate things today? What is going well? What are you doing? What is the next thing you need to do to improve things by 1 or 2 points?

Miracle question

Imagine tonight while you are asleep a miracle happens and this problem is solved. How will you be able to tell the next day that a miracle has happened? No matter how small it is, start tomorrow 'as if' the miracle has happened.

Problem-free talk

Ask the student to speak for a minute about a hobby/interest he or she has. Use this to build a relationship as well as noting his/her skills and personal qualities.

The Columbo technique

Practise 'strategic incompetence'. Ask the student, 'Have you any ideas as to what might help?'

Motivational Equity

Too often the students we are trying to involve in learning are in contexts where rewards are determined by achievements. Given that many of these students would define themselves as lacking the ability to achieve, is it any wonder that they make little effort to obtain the rewards?

Motivational Equity (ME) means that *all* have an equal chance of obtaining rewards because the rewards are linked to learning and effort rather than ability and achievement. This is totally in keeping with an inclusive philosophy. Many students with SEBD, for example, are in fact discriminated against because their disability means that they cannot compete on a 'level playing field' with their peers. However ME allows everyone to achieve, irrespective of ability, background or disability.

In classrooms where ME is practised there is not less learning, there is more. The following principles can be used in a classroom, small group or in a one-to-one situation.

ME principles

The work set is always challenging but within the reach of the student. Tasks are made interesting and linked to real life, with the aim of making them as relevant to the individual student as is possible. The problems presented are intended to tap into a learner's curiosity as well as his or her desire to master new skills.

ME has helped to motivate Vimla, for example, who was finding her geography work less than interesting. Her teacher has devised a project for her around one of her key interests – lions. Now Vimla is learning about the places where lions live and how different countries are trying to protect them.

ME is also helping to improve Tim's negative attitude towards his ball skills, which has stopped him from joining in with his friends when football is played at break times. His support assistant has worked out with Tim a number of activities that are improving his hand–eye coordination. Tim is being helped to record his progress and is beginning to see that he can catch and throw better through regular practice. The next step is for him to play ball games with just a few friends.

Recognition is obtained as a result of the effort learners bring to their tasks as well as their originality in posing new questions and creating new solutions. The ways in which recognition is given will vary, but praise, merit points, certificates, choice of activities and so on will be used. The key point is that there are more than enough rewards for all – there is no scarcity or limit on them.

All students come to see that if they participate and make progress they will be recognised/rewarded. There is no discrimination against those who face a range of disabilities which can limit their learning potential if compared to others – they should be compared against themselves. This also benefits able learners. When there are set rewards for set achievements students who can achieve tend only to do as much as is necessary to earn the reward. ME encourages all students to find and fulfil their own learning potential.

Self-belief is developed through emphasising, modelling and reinforcing learners' personal control. Students are encouraged to challenge inappropriate self-beliefs that focus on ability and achievement. In the ME class ability is seen more as a process than a fixed entity; it is the capacity to modify and develop the student's repertoire of skills; it is fluid and dynamic, rather than fixed and static.

Personal responsibility

Failure is often caused by students setting unrealistic goals: either too hard or too easy. By offering support and developing their confidence, ME helps students to set realistic targets and aim for achievements that are within their competency range. This immediately increases the chance of success and reinforces new beliefs within the student. Nothing breeds success like success. For many students we need to help them overcome their learned fear of success as much as their learned fear of failure.

A case study

At 10 years old, Martin, who has learning difficulties, was causing serious concern to his teacher. His school records showed his behaviour deteriorating as the school year progressed. In class he seemed to be constantly on the move, rarely completing any piece of work without some form of reprimand from his teacher. His impulsiveness meant that he acted without thinking, which resulted in him interfering with other pupils who were working.

Investigations suggested that Martin has few good role models at home, and he has been spotted in the local town mixing with older children who have a history of truanting.

When interviewed about his behaviour and poor attitude towards learning Martin displayed mixed feelings. He seemed to want to do better but said that he found the work either too hard or just boring.

Interventions

His class teacher took a multifaceted approach and employed the following ME strategies:

- Through exploring Martin's interests work was set in the following areas to draw on his natural curiosity:
  – reptiles – Martin had a pet terrapin
  – art – Martin was a good drawer, especially of cartoon characters.
- A positive self-belief was encouraged through Martin producing a photo collage of his work for display in the reception area.
- He also kept a diary, with the help of a support assistant, of the targets he set himself each day and how he solved any difficulties in meeting those targets.
- In class Martin was given a small number of activities – read a book, tidy up the play area, etc. – to do whenever he felt he needed a rest from the work he was doing.
- At all times school staff focused on those times when Martin was engaged with learning and behaving appropriately, for which there was a range of positive consequences. A points system had been devised, with Martin, which enabled

him to choose from a menu of rewards. These ranged from low-level rewards, such as choosing who he could sit with, to *Winner* certificates to take home.

Outcome

At first progress was slow. Martin seemed to find all the increased attention difficult to cope with. However with caring persistence his work output increased and his in-class behaviour improved. While difficult days did occur they were gradually becoming fewer. When last interviewed Martin spoke about the increased number of rewards he was receiving and how he felt he was getting on better with his classmates.

And finally

There will of course be those who will say that this degree of flexibility to meet the needs of one pupil is unfair. What about the attention and time that is being taken away from the other pupils? But surely if we treated all pupils as if they were the same then that would be unfair. Some pupils need individual programmes such as Martin's to motivate them to succeed. Being fair is about enabling all children to be included and achieve their potential. Martin was not getting more than he needed, he was getting what he needed. Other children at other times have different needs.

Further reading

Reference

Miller, R. and Rollnick, S. (1991) *Motivational interviewing*. New York: The Guilford Press.

Recommended reading

Brophy, J. (1998) *Motivating students to learn*. New York: McGraw-Hill.

Burden, P. R. (2000) *Powerful classroom management strategies: motivating students to learn*. Thousand Oaks, California: Corwin Press Inc.

Dreikurs, R., Grunwald, B. and Pepper, F. (1998) *Maintaining sanity in the classroom: classroom management techniques*. London: Accelerated Development.

Galloway, D., Rogers, C., Armstrong, D. and Leo, E. (1998) *Motivating the difficult to reach*. London: Longman.

McNamara, E. (1998) *Motivational interviewing*. Positive Behaviour Management. Available from: 7 Quinton Close, Ainsdale, Merseyside PR8 2TD.

Pintrich, P. and Schunk, D. (1996) *Motivation in education*. Englewood Cliffs, New Jersey: Prentice Hall.

Riding, R. and Rayner, S. (1998) *Cognitive styles & learning strategies*. London: David Fulton.

Selekman, M. (1993) *Pathways to change*. New York: The Guilford Press.

Sommers-Flanagan, J. and Sommers-Flanagan, R. (1997) *Tough kids cool counselling*. Alexandria, USA: American Counseling Association.

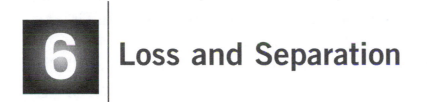

6 Loss and Separation

Understanding loss

> We are healed of a suffering only by experiencing it to the full.
>
> (Proust, *Albertine disparue*, 1925)

The pain caused by loss is not something that some endure and others escape. We all experience it at some time or other and in different ways, whether it is the huge loss at the death of someone we love or the smaller losses such as the loss of a favourite toy or a friend moving away. Loss is a natural part of life and our reactions to it are equally normal. Children experience different types of loss just as adults do – at home, in the classroom, playground and the community.

This chapter will:

- present a model of loss
- provide an *aide-mémoire* for listening to troubled children
- detail the reactions that children have to the loss of a parent.

It will increase awareness of the meaning of loss to children and show school staff why being there is the essential component of any support we can give a child experiencing the pain caused by loss. But it does not offer simplistic solutions to the emotional reactions which are part of the normal healing process.

There will be rare but extreme and traumatic instances where we will need to turn immediately to external colleagues for advice and support. Such circumstances are when children:

- witness murder
- discover a suicidal parent's body
- talk of self-harm.

We are concerned here, however, with how children cope with the more common instances of loss such as when a parent or carer leaves home or when someone close to them dies.

The key assumption here is that the distress that children experience when a family member dies or when the family breaks down will in some way affect their learning and school life. Because schools are so much part of a child's life it follows that there will be times when a child might wish to talk with someone in school. An understanding of some of the processes and reactions to loss will also enable a school to respond sensitively to any changes in a child's behaviour, attitude or general progress.

As a society it has taken us some time to understand and appreciate the fact that children experience the pain of loss as much as adults do. Children grieve in a different way, and at times they may disguise their grief, but they all have reactions to loss, whether big or small.

This chapter is mostly concerned with the 'big losses' that many children face, namely the death of a grandparent or a parent, and the physical loss of a parent through family breakdown. But it should be emphasised that there are other losses that many children face.

Everyday losses

Children show reactions to a wide range of everyday losses that they experience. In school, examples are:

- when a support/care team member moves
- when a child changes class
- when a friend moves away
- when a child unexpectedly fails a test.

At home, examples are:

- the death of a pet
- the loss of favourite toy
- moving to a new area.

Children with special educational needs struggle with and come to terms with loss each day:

- the child suffering with dyslexia feels the loss of not being able to do what his or her peers find so easy
- the child with physical challenges struggles to keep up with his or her friends
- the child with a hearing impairment feels the loss of not understanding or being understood.

While there is no intention here to argue that school staff should be counsellors, all of us have some everyday understanding of loss. However, this understanding is naturally coloured by our own background – which can contain myths that may be less than helpful (such as the belief that it is best to protect children from the pain of loss). Through exploring the meaning and experience of loss this chapter will help an adult sit a little more confidently with a child who is coping with a loss.

Attachment and loss

We cannot understand loss without first exploring attachment. As infants our survival depends upon an adult taking care of us and to ensure this takes place we are all pre-programmed to attach to a carer. The baby is ready to bond with its carer, while the carer is pre-wired to respond to the needs of a baby. A baby has the innate capacity to communicate its needs: a cry can produce an immediate reaction. Without immediate care babies would be in extreme danger of perishing.

A major contributor to our understanding of the attachment process is John Bowlby (quoted in Holmes, 1995). Bowlby argued that infants are pre-programmed with attachment behaviour which is aimed at maintaining the strong emotional and physical bond between mother and child. Some examples would be clinging to the mother and crying when separated.

BUT when this natural biological bond is broken there are set reactions that occur. This was first detailed in the work of Robertson (Robertson, 1952), a colleague of John Bowlby. Robertson filmed and detailed the reactions of infants when separated from their parents due to hospitalisation. He identified three distinct phases.

- *Phase 1*: Strong reaction, aggressively tearful. The behaviour is attempting to re-establish the relationship as it was.
- *Phase 2*: A mournful period follows. Here the child seems to be grieving the loss.
- *Phase 3*: In this phase the child seems to return to a near normal state where he or she is now able to cope with the loss and continue with his or her life.

There seems to be a natural process that occurs when the biological bond is broken. The first stage is an attempt to re-establish the bond. There is an anger that drives the child and his or her crying is of an angry, screaming type.

If the relationship cannot be re-established there is a 'mourning'-type reaction to the loss, when sadness becomes the dominant emotional response. This phase

133

involves the beginnings of an acceptance of the loss. The crying that occurs now is a much deeper type; the child sobs.

Finally the child moves towards the acceptance of the loss and develops ways of adjusting to a world without the loved one. There is not a 'getting over' the loss, but a coping. We talk of our heart 'being shattered'. This seems to describe how we fall apart and then come back together in a different way now that our world has changed.

One cannot imagine losing a loved person and not having a strong emotional reaction. It would be psychologically contradictory to say that we loved someone and felt nothing at the loss of them. The price of loving is the pain that we feel at their loss.

The reactions that this model suggest are presented in Figure 6.1.

While this model specifically increases our understanding of how children react to loss through bereavement, it can serve as a useful framework to understand many other losses. The loss of a parent through family breakdown does not have the finality of bereavement, but a child's reaction to it will share many similarities. For example, a child whose father was tragically killed in a farm accident became much more argumentative and disobedient at school, while a girl of eight whose parents were in the middle of an acrimonious divorce became extremely sullen, despondent and complained of being frequently tired. For both children these behaviours were not typical.

STAGE	Protest	Despair	Adjust
Feelings	shock anger denial	sadness, confusion, longing	becoming to terms
Behaviour	arguments and disobedience	tearfulness, loss of sleep and appetite	new friends and activities
Thoughts	I cannot imagine life without them	If only... I would do anything to bring them back	I am still sad, but I can cope
TASK	Accept loss	Experience grief	Adjust and cope

FIGURE 6.1 Making sense of loss

If the reactions are natural, why do children need help? Given that the responses seem to be biologically programmed into us, why do so many children and adults experience difficulties in expressing their grief? The answer lies in the way we are socialised through our family into the dominant cultural values of our time. This is how we learn to avoid emotions that need to be expressed. A useful way to understand this is to think of all of the 'cultural myths' that we learn which are supposed to deal with our emotions, such as:

- be strong
- time will heal
- cheer up
- grieve alone.

The result of these is that many of us find it hard to express how we actually feel. These emotions can then knot up inside and lead to such negative results as:

- behaviour problems
- phobias
- physical illness.

Models of loss

There have been many ways of making sense of severe loss. In the past loss was often seen as a 'one-off' event that children recovered from as well as they could. More recently this was modified to include an understanding of the 'aftershocks' that are felt many times after the actual loss; for example, when a child has to cope with Special Days.

Today it is accepted that significant losses reverberate throughout a person's life. Severe losses in childhood can change the direction in which a child is developing. A lively, outgoing child can become passive and withdrawn if a number of losses are experienced close together. The child's developing personality can be altered in the face of such painful and uncontrollable events. This emphasises the profound effect early losses can have on children and the importance of the way in which they are supported to help them tolerate the sadness the loss causes and to go on to function competently in the real world.

We must remember that the model shown in Figure 1 is a framework to help us understand the process of loss and is not meant to be imposed on children. The experience of grief needs best to be seen as a journey. Some will pass through it relatively quickly. Others will go around roundabouts many times, sometimes

135

entering a cul-de-sac. The average time for a child to come to terms with a significant loss is two years.

Children's reactions to loss

There are some common general reactions to loss which might include:

- behavioural problems
- aggressive behaviour
- eating/sleep disorders
- psychosomatic disorders
- attempts to replace lost person
- adopting mannerisms of lost person.

Children sometimes employ defence mechanisms which are intended to protect their self-esteem from experiences that are painful. Such defences are seen in the type of behaviours observed. They include:

- regression; for example, bedwetting
- denial
- withdrawal
- acting out – fighting
- acting in – withdrawal.

The range of emotions they are experiencing can include:

- guilt – was it something I said or did that made them go?
- anxiety – one parent has left me; will the other one leave me too?
- anger – how dare they change my life and turn my world upside down?
- sorrow – will my life ever be the same again?

Their pain displays itself through changes in their behaviour at school such as:

- learning difficulties
- restlessness
- daydreaming, poor concentration
- withdrawal
- peer relationship difficulties
- over-sensitivity to criticism

- deterioration in achievement
- delinquency.

It is important to note that basically any change in a child's normal pattern of behaviour can be a reaction to loss. There are no definitive symptoms; we each grieve in our own unique way. Our reactions to loss may be seen as a 'healing process'. Just as when we cut ourselves there is a process by which our body heals itself, so it is with emotional pain.

There is no cure for the pain that children experience. Our aim in offering help is to enable them to develop age-appropriate understanding that what they are feeling is a normal reaction. When children have intense emotional reactions it can be very scary: 'Is it normal to feel like this?' Our role can be to help them to face the painful reality at their own pace – not ours.

Listening to troubled children

Before exploring some of the skills we need in order to truly listen to children we need to be aware of the many factors which will influence the type of response a child has to loss. The more we can appreciate these, the more we can appreciate the complexity of a child's reactions.

Within-child factors

As a child's thinking abilities develop, the understanding they have of loss and death affects the way in which we talk to them. We need to provide information at a level that makes sense to them. Some of the factors that affect a child's reaction to loss are:

- age
- personality
- gender
- previous experiences
- closeness of relationship
- type of loss – sudden vs. anticipated
- expression of 'farewell'.

Listening and talking

Listening and talking to troubled children is something that we can all do. The following is intended as an aide-mémoire to the core skills that can help encourage a troubled child to talk to us and enable us to listen more effectively.

Do

- answer those questions that are asked
- answer questions immediately
- accept their feelings
- accept answers given
- if you don't know, say so
- say, 'Would you like to talk? I'll listen.'
- talk about feelings of guilt – 'If only'
- keep decision-making to a minimum
- remember special days; send a note
- help organise evenings and weekends with clubs and trips to ensure they have a focus and not just unstructured free time.

Avoid

- asking 'Do you understand?'
- asking multiple questions
- interrupting
- using closed questions
- saying, 'I know how you feel'
- platitudes – 'You'll get over it in time.'

Children will often be confused and frightened by the emotions they are feeling. Let them know that other children would feel the same. It can be reassuring for a child to know that their emotions are normal.

Soften painful questions. Instead of asking, 'Why did you run out of class?' ask, 'What has happened to make you upset enough to run out of class?'

Give alternatives. 'Some children like to be alone when they are sad; some children want to be with someone else when they are sad. What do you like to do when you are sad?'

Avoid forcing children to deny some undesirable behaviour. Instead of asking, 'Have you ever thought of hurting your sister?' say, 'Tell me about a time when you thought of hurting someone else.'

Allow children the chance to express positive answers before negative ones. 'What do you like best about your new class?' Follow this with 'What do you like least about your new class?'

CASE STUDY: EMMA

Emma is 11 years old and considered by most staff to be immature for her age. In class Emma is generally quiet and mixes with a few close friends. Emma's father had been terminally ill for some time and within the last week died. Since then staff have noticed that Emma is more withdrawn than usual and prone to overreacting to any form of criticism about her work. Her friends have reported that she is very sullen, moody and has been snappy with one of her closest friends.

There is a positive relationship between home and school. Emma has one brother younger than her.

Behaviour in school

Emma is seen by a number of teachers as giving cause for concern. In class her concentration span is poor and most of the time she seems unhappy, depressed and anxious. When confronted about her difficulties she will become snappy and defensive.

Observational information

Whenever we interview a child there is a lot of information available, indicated by their:

- general appearance – are they cared for? Do they care for themselves?
- speech and language – are they able to understand and express ideas?
- interaction skills – does their behaviour indicate social confidence?
- non-verbal information – do they speak with a nervous/depressed/ happy or aggressive tone?

The interview

Phase 1

Emma is clearly distressed at having to talk about her recent bereavement and half expects to be told off about her behaviour. Her helper decides to let her sit quietly and uses a 'sentence completion' task as a way of getting to know her better and to help her relax.

Some examples used are:

- I like it when ....
- One thing I like about myself is...
- My friends like me because ....
- A happy memory I have is of when...
- My favourite colour is...
- A new skill I have learned is...
- My favourite meal is..

Phase 2

The child tells her story

The helper now asks Emma to tell her something about how she would like to be supported during this time in school. Emma is now more settled and begins to explain how much she hates being made to feel different because of her dad's death. It seems that everybody is asking her how she feels all the time. The helper responds with nods and such expressions as 'Ah-ha', 'Uh-hm', 'Yes' or 'Right'. Occasionally she says, 'I see what you mean' or 'I understand.'

At one point Emma says, 'I sometimes feel so angry when my friends tell me I'll be better soon. I know they're only trying to help but it stresses me out.'

The helper replies, 'You sound very frustrated and angry at everyone talking to you about your dad's death and you wish they would leave you alone.' The helper is checking with Emma that she understands what has been said. She is not repeating back what has been said in a parrot-like fashion. She is highlighting some of the key points that have been made.

Later Emma says that most of the time when she arrives home from school there is no one there, her mother having gone to fetch her little brother. It feels sometimes that he has all the time with Mum and that she is left out. The helper responds, 'It sounds as if your mum isn't around for you very often.'

140

Like most of us, children would often prefer to avoid exploring painful feelings. Therefore, while some children will be open, many will seek to avoid painful memories. The more we are tuned in to a child then the easier it is for us to detect their feelings. If we correctly pick up their key feelings we can help them consciously to recognise how they are feeling. It is through increasing the child's awareness and understanding that they are able to learn to accept their negative feelings and to find more positive ways of controlling and/or expressing them.

These two processes can be combined. For example, when Emma says, 'At home it's always my little brother who gets the attention; it isn't fair', the helper says, 'It sounds as if it makes you angry to see your mum giving more time to his needs than to yours.'

There are times when Emma seems to get stuck in telling her story. At such times the helper tries to help by prompting Emma to give a full description such as, 'Tell me some of the happy memories you have of your dad,' rather than asking questions that just lead to 'yes' or 'no' answers. When the helper asks, 'If you could say one thing to your dad, what would it be?' Emma responds very quickly with 'Sorry'. Further exploration shows that Emma's dad died after she woke him up playing her music. For Emma, if she hadn't done this he might still be alive.

It is not uncommon for children to implicate themselves in such painful events. They reverse to a magical thinking stage. This is the tendency for children to believe that they can make things happen just by thinking about them, or that any event that follows an action of theirs is caused by them. Thus the death of Emma's father followed her waking him up.

At times the helper feels overwhelmed by the amount of information Emma is offering and she tries to draw the key points that are being made together. 'It seems to me, Emma, that there are two main concerns that are troubling you. Firstly, at home you don't feel you are being treated as fairly or receiving as much attention from your mum as your brother is and, secondly, you feel guilty about waking your dad up on the day he died. Have I missed anything out?'

The helper is now able to focus attention on helping Emma to manage her irrational thoughts about the cause of her dad's death, and she plans to meet with Mum to improve the support Emma is receiving at home.

A MODEL OF CHANGE

Listening to children

When we are working with children it is good if we have some kind of mental template to help us support them more effectively. This can prevent us from going around in circles and feeling at a loss as to what we should do next. The model below is a template. It will not always fit your approach but it may help you keep focused.

Phase 1

Joining together
This is the stage where a relationship is developed to enable the child to feel safe and secure. Being at the same eye level as the child will be less threatening; sitting alongside rather than directly opposite is less confrontational. Using a similar response speed to the child when speaking will also help develop an emotionally supportive atmosphere.

Phase 2

Story-telling
Now the child begins to tell their story. They may do this through language, through playing with toys, drawing or puppets. Your task is to help them find the media that suits them.

Phase 3

Awareness and insight
This will obviously depend on the cognitive ability of the child. But if you can help a child develop insight into the causes of their difficulties then this will help in their motivation to change. The child here is in touch with strong negative emotions. In this phase you will help the child challenge negative self-beliefs they may have as well as understanding that their emotions are normal. Children who experience several rejections can come to believe that they are unlovable. This can be gently challenged by exploring their existing friendships and discussing the positive qualities that their friends see in them.

Phase 4

Options and choices
The child can now be helped to look for solutions or ways of coping more effectively. It is helpful to look at what they might have already tried. Often

children have the right solution but don't persist with it. For example, a child might have asked a friend to come for tea one evening and, because their friend was unable to – due to existing commitments – they feel rejected and give up trying.

Phase 5

Practice

Make sure the child has time and opportunities to practise the new thinking or behavioural skills needed. Remember they may be trying to break over-learned patterns of behaviour that have helped them cope. Such behaviours could include avoiding certain situations or people or becoming more passive and withdrawn. Habits do not change just because we wish them to.

Phase 6

Adaptive functioning

Your meetings with the child have successfully enabled them to understand why they felt like they did and why they behaved as they did. They now have better ways of coping with their thoughts and feelings.

REMEMBER
RESISTANCE, WITHDRAWAL, AVOIDANCE AND DENIAL ARE NORMAL.

As you help to bring issues into a child's awareness, strong negative emotions could well emerge, such as:

● sadness about the loss

● anger through rejection or envy

● anxiety through fear of loneliness.

While many children will have the psychological ability to face these emotions and to take control through understanding them, there will also be many who will block them off. When this happens it may help to change the medium that you are using. For example, they may not be able to tell their story through words. Explore alternatives, such as music, poetry, play, art, etc. Kuli, for example, was very keen on music and this was used to explore his emotions by finding songs that related to his sadness and his anger. Alternatively, if the young person follows a TV soap, then there may well be characters that they identify with and these can be used to help explore their feelings and attitudes in a way that makes sense to them. Your aim is to find a means of enabling the child to join with you to tell their story.

(Note: always remember that we are trying to be a skilled helper not a trained bereavement counsellor or Relate counsellor. The more uncertainty you feel about your role the more you should talk with colleagues. Referring on is not a sign of weakness but one of strength – it reflects your genuine care for the child.)

To conclude this chapter there are some final but extremely important points to be made.

Firstly, it is the children who are facing the loss – not us. They will cope through finding those ways that are appropriate for them.

Secondly, they are not sick or disturbed. They are facing what humanity has faced throughout all time. We suffer from an over-professionalisation of core human experiences – they have been taken over by experts. There is a risk of us talking about the children's need for therapy or counselling when in reality they need someone to help them find their way on their journey. We do not need formal training to listen in a caring and supportive way to a child in distress – if we do need formal therapy we have allowed ourselves to be deskilled in our ability to care for each other.

A child who has lost someone they cared for is in search of making sense of a new world, a world without the loved one. They need support, not therapy.

Bereavement

Children's understanding of death

How children respond to the death of a parent will depend on many factors, some of which have already been detailed in Chapter 1. The child's cognitive level of understanding of death is, though, one of the most important factors and will significantly determine their reactions. The role of the media cannot be underestimated in this area; many children will be seeing and learning about death via the TV soaps.

The different levels of understanding about death can be broadly assumed by age:

Birth to seven

For the very young death is synonymous with 'away' or 'out of sight, out of mind'. Providing the child has someone else they are attached to then the loss can be minimised. A child's love is not finite – they can be attached to many people.

However, during this stage the child has 'magical thinking'. Their egocentricism leads them to believe that they can make things happen – just by thinking. They can as a result have irrational thoughts which can cause emotional difficulties. For example, if a grandparent dies after an argument with a child, the child can feel responsible. Similarly they may think that they can wish someone alive again.

Seven to adolescence

Children now become more aware of the finality of death. A child's ability to deal with the severe emotional pain of loss is far less than an adult's. As a result they may:

- deny the hurt and show opposite feelings, seem to be happy
- displace their painful feelings on to another less significant event, they may overreact to the death of a pet, allowing the release of their pain
- have obsessional thoughts to do with death and funerals, etc.; for example, may visit a grave frequently and talk of joining the loved one
- have aggressive outbursts that release emotions and generate attention
- isolate themselves and withdraw from usual activities
- develop emotional and physical symptoms, such as anxiety at going to school, headaches and a loss of appetite.

Behavioural reactions

Children will often try various ways of coping, some of which are less than helpful over a long period.

- *substitution* – a child may strongly and quickly attach to a substitute mother or father
- *aggression* – a child may become unmanageable at home and fight and truant at school; a general pattern of discipline and antisocial problems may begin to emerge
- *withdrawal* – a child may lose their drive and curiosity towards life in general; their learning suffers and they develop a poor self-esteem and a 'what's the point?' attitude; they can become apathetic and socially isolated.

Why is grieving healthy?

Strong feelings of attachment and fear of abandonment are part of our biological inheritance. Through experiencing the mixture of emotions that loss causes, anger as well as sadness, we are able to move on to develop adaptive ways of coping.

What is complicated grief?

Sometimes powerful emotions are held within. When any relationship ends there are often mixed emotions. If the child has learned to suppress certain emotions, 'be strong, don't cry', they may try to suppress their feelings. But feelings do not go away – they seek release either through behaviour or physical symptoms. These emotional knots will require professional help.

When should I refer on?

Some of the signs that should lead us to referring on include when a bereaved child:

- is acting as if nothing has happened
- denies that anyone has died
- threatens or talks of suicide
- becomes persistently aggressive
- becomes withdrawn and socially isolated
- becomes involved in antisocial behaviour – drugs, stealing, etc.

> **REMEMBER**
> **IF SUICIDE WAS THE CAUSE OF DEATH, THIS CAN BE ESPECIALLY DIFFICULT FOR A CHILD TO UNDERSTAND AND COPE WITH.**

How can schools help?

Most children have a fear of being made to feel different. They have a strong desire to be similar to their peers. Any support needs to be sensitive and aware of this. A child who is grieving has the following tasks:

- to accept the loss
- to express his or her feelings

- to accept his or her feelings as normal
- to live independently without the loved one.

Returning to school after a bereavement can be stressful for children. While for some school can offer both relief and security from an overwhelmingly painful atmosphere of home, for others it increases their anxiety about the grieving parent left, perhaps alone, at home. A grieving child will be wondering how their peers and teachers are going to react to them.

Helping a child return to school after a bereavement

The skilled helper supports a child from the stage they have reached with regard to their emotions and self-understanding. Help is:

- not assuming that a child can cope without support
- being open, honest and available but not pushy
- talking about good and bad memories
- accepting a child's feelings
- writing poems, letters or songs to the loved one
- drawing pictures, or making up stories about/for the loved one
- going over final farewells, or establishing some final goodbye
- being a good listener, being there if needed
- accepting all questions without feeling the need to answer the unanswerable ones – 'I don't know' is an honest answer
- offering time to be with the child; brief but regular meetings can mean a lot to a child and being offered help is the best antidote to the fear of loneliness and rejection which a child may be feeling
- helping the child to find those friends who can be supportive
- removing unnecessary responsibilities
- modelling healthy coping strategies
- avoiding clichés such as 'You've got to be strong', 'You seem to be coping so well', 'You're the man of the house now', etc.

Ongoing support

Because all children are different and the cultures of their schools will differ also, there can be no checklist of 'things to do'. What feels right for one child in one school might not for another. The additional ideas presented here reflect this:

- establish peer support by asking the child if they have a close friend they would like to be with

- use literature, music and poetry to help a child develop an awareness and understanding of the normal human responses to pain and loss

- give permission for child to express feelings – tears are OK

- give time and attention

- listen

- tackle the taboo by being open and prepared to discuss death and family breakdown in assemblies and during circle time. If there are 'sad' events known to many children, then ensure that these are formally recognised and respected

- watch for behaviour changes

- involve child's special friends

- be honest in answering their questions

- don't deny their viewpoint

- be mindful of special days

- be aware of previous bereavements

- maintain self-esteem by encouraging the continuation of routines – seeing friends, etc.

- provide bolt-holes, such as a place in the library, where the child can go to

- keep child with peers

- be sensitive to a child's beliefs

- offer concentration strategies

- do picture stories; if a child is happy drawing, then support them in recreating special memories of holidays and trips, for example

- create a special album which could include a wide range of memories and photographs

- let them know that their thoughts and feelings are normal

- form a support circle open to all children, where an understanding of loss and our emotional reactions could be taught and ways of coping developed

- make a memorial, perhaps by creating a flower-bed or planting a tree

- encourage them to keep a journal to help them deal with their feelings

- write an account which could be shared if they chose to

- encourage them to join a local support group, such as CRUSE.

The best way to support any child is to listen and be guided by how they would like to be supported.

> **REMEMBER**
> **ALWAYS KEEP IN TOUCH WITH THE FAMILY.**

Family separation

Being brought up by a single parent, Mum or Dad, is not in itself a problem for children. For many it can be a positive experience. It is how the family breaks down and how the parents relate to each other after the separation that matters most. Twenty-eight per cent of the calls received by ChildLine are from children whose parents are not getting on well. Children are affected by family discord in a number of ways:

- they become distressed by the negative feelings it causes in them
- they become aggressive as they imitate their parents' behaviour
- they become unmanageable as a way of distracting their parents from their conflict.

Each of these has implications for how children behave in school. An indirect impact on children stems from the way in which problems between the adults can spill over into problems in the parent–child relationship. Parents caught up in hostile relationships may turn their anger towards their children. Their parenting skills are also likely to be under stress. Children may also relate back in a reciprocal manner to their parents.

SEPARATION = CHANGE

When families break down children experience many changes. Some are of a practical kind. Separation might mean:

- moving house
- changing school – having to make new friends
- new routines
- a different standard of living
- losing touch with extended family and friends
- remaining parent may now work
- new responsibilities at home.

Also separation can cause emotional changes, such as:

- feeling very sad
- becoming very angry
- missing one parent
- wanting to blame someone
- anxiety about the future
- worry about departed parent
- fear of being left by remaining parent
- coping with parents' emotions and behaviours
- divided loyalties.

Separation is an adult solution to the problem of an unhappy relationship. But from a child's point of view the adult is not just leaving his or her partner, they are leaving the family. Children can have many questions:

- where has Mummy/Daddy gone?
- why did they split up?
- will they be able to cope on their own?
- will they ever come back?
- was it my fault?
- do they still love me?
- is divorce catching – will it happen to me?
- will they still love me if they find a new partner and have new children?

Some of the emotional reactions a child might experience when a family is breaking up include:

Phase 1. Uncertainty

Family stability is threatened by discord. Children are unsure as to what will happen to them. They can feel forced to keep family secrets. They may be passive observers or become actively involved.

Emotional distress
There can be a reawakening of a child's separation anxiety from early childhood. They can have mood swings.

School behaviour

They can become over-sensitive to criticism. Their ability to concentrate diminishes and their learning will begin to suffer as emotional energy is diverted to protect self and others.

Phase 2. Denial

Children can now feel torn between their loyalties to each parent. They will act 'as if' matters were OK. They will not wish to talk about difficulties as this will make them real. They will manifest aspects of magical thinking: 'If I don't talk about it, it is not happening.'

Emotional distress

Children can experience feelings of guilt about whether or not they caused their parents to separate. Self-punishment can occur in the form of self-injurious behaviour, such as cutting, scratching and bruising themselves. The pain seems to give relief from the pain inside. Their distress can lead to nightmares as well as a lack of self-care, poor appetite, etc.

School behaviour

There might be a tendency to become isolated from others, to have little energy for new ventures and to avoid taking on responsibilities.

Phase 3. Anger

The fear of being seen to be different from others, along with a change in personal status, can lead to strong expressions of anger. They can become hostile towards the perceived guilty parent.

Emotional distress

Pent-up anger may be turned outwards by showing anger towards other children; this is in effect envy at their apparent happy family lives. Or the anger can be turned in on the self in the form of extreme submissiveness, as seen in the child who no longer initiates conversations with friends and seems to expect to be left out of activities.

School behaviour

Children can become emotionally volatile and prone to sudden outbursts in the classroom. Small frustrations trigger off excessive reactions.

151

Phase 4. Despair

There is a loss of pleasure in activities that they used to enjoy. They may no longer enjoy their usual TV programmes and they respond coolly to trips that were once welcomed. There is a realisation that reunion of their family is unlikely. The child's growing sense of acceptance brings grief-like reactions.

Emotional distress

There is a tendency for children in this phase to suffer psychosomatic illnesses such as stomach pains and headaches – as if they search for increased nurture. Regressive behaviours such as bedwetting and clinginess may also emerge. Again, these are behaviours that seek to elicit increased support at a time of sorrow.

School behaviour

Responses more appropriate to the child when younger can develop. They may cry at minor setbacks and run out of lessons when reprimanded.

Phase 5. Coping

The child is now coming to terms with a new 'normality'. They have acquired a new identity.

Emotional distress

There can be apprehensiveness about a parent developing new relationships.

School behaviour

They develop a more open-minded approach and a willingness to explore alternative solutions and become less rigid in their thinking, returning to their thinking style prior to the loss. They are more optimistic about the future and will, for example, be less critical of the parent who left the family home.

Supporting children in school

When talking with children it is important to bear in mind that their reactions to separation vary according to their age and the support they are given should be appropriate to their level of development.

Reactions and support by age

Preschool

Children of this age have limited understanding and will often escape into fantasy. They may regress and lose skills they had mastered. Bedwetting may start and nightmares are not uncommon. They may show signs of anxiety about meeting the other parent. Their sleep and eating patterns might change.

At this age children need brief and clear instructions and explanations. Routines are very important and extra comforters such as cuddles and security toys matter a lot.

Primary

Children now experience worries about losing their family. They can experience intense sadness and they can also feel angry at being left by one parent. They can become involved in taking messages between their parents. In school they can become disorganised and may be aggressive towards authority figures.

Questions now need to be answered sensitively and regular opportunities made to allow the child to talk if he or she wishes.

Secondary

Children can now become extremely embarrassed about the change in their family. They often have strong ideas about right and wrong and may well see one parent as being to blame. They may cope by throwing themselves into schoolwork or activities as a way of avoiding the painful reality.

Children need to have their worries accepted and to be reassured that their reactions are normal. Any behavioural problems need to be treated in a matter-of-fact manner.

General

All children will suffer from a sense of helplessness. They are at risk of feeling out of control and that nothing they do can make a difference; for example, when parents try to involve them in arrangements they seem uninterested. While there are many aspects of separation that are naturally beyond their control it is important to help children appreciate those aspects of their lives where they do have control, such as organising their weekend activities, meeting with friends, clothes, etc.

Further reading

References

Holmes, J. (1995) *John Bowlby and Attachment Theory*. London: Routledge.

Robertson, J. (1952) Film: *A Two-Year-Old Goes to Hospital*. London: Tavistock.

Recommended reading

Atkinson, M. and Hornby, G. (2002) *Mental Health Handbook for Schools*. London: Routledge Falmer.

Ayalon, O. and Flasher, A. (1993) *Chain Reaction: Children and Divorce*. London: Jessica Kingsley Publishers.

Boyd Webb, N. (1993) *Helping Bereaved Children*. New York: The Guilford Press.

Cox, K. and Desforges, M. (1987) *Divorce and the School*. London: Methuen.

James, J. and Friedman, R. (2001) *When Children Grieve*. New York: HarperCollins Publishers.

Jewett, C. (1982) *Helping Children Cope with Separation and Loss*. London: Batsford.

Reynolds, J. (2001) *Not in Front of the Children?* London: One Plus One.

Sharp, S. and Cowie, H. (1998) *Counselling and Supporting Children in Distress*. London: SAGE.

Contacts

CRUSE: a charitable organisation offering bereavement counselling, training workshops and publications.

www:crusebereavementcare.org.uk

helpline: 0870 167 1677

Obsessive Compulsive Disorders

Introduction

All children experience situations that naturally make them feel frightened and upset. Up until the age of two, separation anxiety is one such situation, when children become distressed if separated from their carers. This is a normal emotional reaction and is no indication of future problems (in fact it is more a sign for concern when a child does not show any anxiety at being separated). By the age of two, however, most children are able to cope with being out of sight of their carer for short periods of time.

At different ages there are certain 'behavioural rituals' that, while suggestive of OCD, are actually a part of normal development. These may include cuddling favourite toys or blankets when faced with new situations. This would not be unusual for a three-year-old child. However, when a child of eight or nine still experiences the same need, and is anxious if he or she cannot carry out the same routine as before, then this response may be a problem and the child will need understanding and support. As Kendall (2000) puts it, 'there are different fears for different years' – the behaviour is normal for the three-year-old but less so for the eight-year-old.

Common childhood fears and anxieties

Eight months to two years
Separation anxiety – common rituals exist around bedtimes; for example, some children always need the same soft toys placed in the same order.

Two to four years
Imaginary fears – the dark, animals; mild forms of checking such as making sure windows are securely closed; fear of germs and dirt.

Six years on

Fears of injury, death and natural disasters; counting (for example, always counting to a certain number while they are getting dressed) and lucky numbers.

(Kendall, 2000; Thomsen, 2001)

It is common for children aged two or above to develop their own patterns of ritual. Bedtimes are a good example, with children demanding that the same book or page be read even though more interesting stories are available. We can see this as children's way of coping with anxieties – the rituals serve to comfort and distract them from worries. As they grow they develop new and different ways of coping. As with many behaviours there is a continuum which shows this to be normal in certain contexts and at certain stages of development. It is when the behaviour continues into different contexts and/or different ages that it becomes dysfunctional and prevents the child from adapting successfully.

Anxiety and fear are natural, unlearned reactions that warn us that something is not right. They signal a need for action to avoid some threat. But there will be occasions when they are the cause of problems: they can be associated with situations that were previously neutral but come to trigger alarm and fear responses. Thoughts and images, such as of a parent having an accident, can lead to anxiety. In OCD compulsive behaviours are used to allay or reduce the anxiety. The result is that as the anxiety is reduced the behaviour is reinforced and becomes even more resistant to change.

Repetitive and negative obsessions

Adela

Adela was accidentally pushed over in the playground and needed attention to a badly cut knee. For a short period she remained in school during break times. The day she returned to the playground coincided with a violent thunderstorm that frightened all the children. But for Adela it once again meant that she experienced fear in the playground. Staff began to notice that she was reluctant to leave the classroom at break times and seemed to look for any reason whatsoever not to go out.

Adela was beginning to develop a 'phobic reaction' to the playground. A phobia can be defined as the avoidance of a specific situation/event and thus the negative experience of anxiety. As long as she stayed away from the playground Adela did not have to face the situation that caused her anxiety, thereby reinforcing the avoiding behaviour.

Children with OCD usually have a degree of insight into the negative aspects of their thoughts and behaviours. This is referred to as ego-dystonic, meaning that the self regards these thoughts and behaviours as repugnant or inconsistent with the view the individual holds of himself or herself. This is why these children can be so secretive about what they do: they are embarrassed and ashamed because they know their behaviour is not 'normal'.

Because every child has a unique nervous system his or her emotional reactions to the fears he or she face will vary. Some children are more temperamentally disposed to anxiety than others. Being vulnerable, though, does not mean that the child will necessarily develop an anxiety-based psychological disorder.

Imran

Imran was 10 years old and preferred to walk to school with his sister than his friends. This was acceptable until his sister began to complain. Imran became upset and defiant if he was asked to go with anyone else. What seemed to be a childhood preference was beginning to turn into a problem. During playtimes he would seek out his sister to play with. He was becoming more and more isolated from his own peers.

His parents met with his class teacher and over a period of time Imran was helped to rely more on his friends for company. This was achieved through such techniques as providing Imran with a 'break time buddy' and teaching him relaxation skills alongside his peers.

You could argue that if Imran's parents and school staff had not been sensitive to his personality then he could well have developed an excessive reliance on his sister, which would have resulted in further difficulties as he moved towards secondary school transfer.

Obsessive compulsive disorder (OCD)

OCD is a condition characterised by recurring obsessive thoughts and/or compulsive actions. We all have some aspect of this disorder but, because we are able to keep the thoughts and behaviours in check, they do not interfere with our daily lives. Some of us have unpleasant or frightening thoughts that keep intruding. We are able to prevent them taking control over us, however – we are aware that they are irrational and should not be given the excessive time and attention that they seem to think they deserve. Others of us are more ritualistic/superstitious in our actions. We may be 'checkers' – we do not check once to see if the gas is turned off, or if the door is locked, but several times. Or we may play the 'symmetrics game' – if we touch one railing as we walk then we feel a compulsion to touch them all ('Step on a crack, break your mother's back', as the old rhyme went).

These patterns of behaviour and thought are common to us all; only a minority of people develop OCD to the point that it dominates and devastates their lives. Famous people, who sadly have the time and money to indulge the disorder, show how disastrous OCD can be if left unchecked. Howard Hughes is perhaps one of the most well-known OCD victims. His obsessive fear of germs, which began in his childhood, led to an adult obsession with cleanliness and ultimately to a sad and lonely life, despite his wealth and fame.

Most adults who suffer with OCD speak of it beginning in their childhood. It is something that they managed alone and often kept secret from their family and friends out of shame and embarrassment. Too often the reaction from others to people with OCD is 'pull yourself together', 'just stop doing it' or 'you really must try harder'. These statements are more of a moral judgement than an understanding of the difficulty – the OCD victim cannot just stop the behaviour any more than you or I can stop breathing. OCD is a disorder over which the individual is incapable of simply taking control without support and skills training.

In most schools there will be a few children who display the disorder. OCD has two aspects:

1 Obsessive thoughts
2 Compulsive behaviours.

Obsessive thoughts

These are usually ideas, pictures or impulses which are upsetting to the individual, who tries to repress them. Even though they are involuntary, the sufferer believes that he or she has no control over them. They are usually unpleasant, silly or embarrassing and they keep coming back, time after time.

Compulsive behaviours

These are actions that have to be done to a degree that is beyond their usefulness. Hand washing is sensible until taken to such an extreme that other activities are prevented. If the actions are not performed the child can feel worried, angry and frustrated. These 'magical' actions are undertaken as a way of avoiding some unpleasant consequence – the fear of dirt and germs can result in a pattern of compulsive hand washing.

While it is possible to have either the obsessive thoughts or the compulsive behaviours alone it is more common for them to coexist.

The following data were obtained from children and young people around the world who were diagnosed as having OCD. Thomsen (2001) found no gender differences.

Obsessive thoughts towards	Seen in % of the survey group
Dirt and contamination	40
Fear of something terrible happening	20
Illness	20
Death	20
Symmetry	15
Sex	10
Religion	10
Self-injury	8

These statistics show some of the commonest symptoms that children and young people with OCD display, but they fail to relay the depth and misery that OCD leads to. Thomsen (2001) describes the following two cases of OCD in children:

> Jane phones home some 40 times a day because of her fear that something bad has happened to her mother. The phone call (a compulsive behaviour) gives her immediate short-term relief as she speaks to her mother. But the obsessive thought that something bad might have happened since she last rang leads to another phone call to allay her fears. Her thoughts and behaviour are dominated and controlled by the OCD.
>
> John believes that he is responsible for accidents caused to people in the streets where he lives. To allay this anxiety he begins to collect all street rubbish and debris that might cause accidents. But after doing this he worries that he did not collect it all and returns to his compulsive behaviour which is constantly triggered by his illogical thought processes.
>
> (from Thomsen, 2001)

While there have been reports of children as young as three years old showing OCD symptoms, these cases are extremely rare. The illness is typically seen in children between the ages of nine and thirteen. However, the younger the child is at the onset of OCD, the worse the prognosis for recovery (Skoog and Skoog, 1999, in Kendall, 2000). Therefore early intervention is strongly recommended.

What causes OCD?

There are many plausible explanations for OCD and the most influential of these are listed below. While research exists to support each one there is also contra-evidence.

Biological factors

Some researchers believe that OCD is caused by certain nerve impulses failing to control deep-seated behaviours. As a result, instinctive behavioural and thought patterns that relate to safety or grooming are released with no controls.

Yes and ... neurological disorders and OCD are found to happen together when the same areas of the brain are damaged.

Yes but ... why is it that children who have a normal development for a number of years suddenly develop obsessive symptoms? Also, children who suffer from OCD can have significant periods with no symptoms and then suffer a relapse.

Family influences

The families of OCD children can seem to be more rigid, with less flexibility in their parenting patterns than families with no history of OCD. There is often an authoritative style of parenting, with rules being non-negotiable.

Yes and … Adams (1973) found that there was a greater emphasis on cleanliness and perfection in the families of children with OCD.

Yes but … Thomsen (2001) found that there were no significant differences between the parents of children with OCD and other parents whose children had a range of difficulties.

Heredity

Evidence exists to suggest that if parents suffer with OCD then there is an increased probability that their children will also.

Yes and … if one parent has OCD then there is a chance of between two and eight per cent that the children will develop OCD.

Yes but … twin studies have failed to provide conclusive evidence as to whether or not OCD is inherited.

Stress

Parents of children with OCD suggest that their children are prone to anxiety – a common feature of OCD sufferers – and that stressful conditions lead to the development of OCD. Some examples are family breakdown, changing schools, examinations and friendship disputes. Also, the amount of time that the OCD can take up can itself result in the child being under stress to complete all other activities.

Yes and … a 1992 study (Rettew, 1992) found that 38% of patients or their family members believed a specific event preceded their OCD behaviour.

Yes but … Chansky (2000) found that most children reported that they had 'low grade' OCD before a stress trigger led to the full-blown OCD. It seems likely that, while stress does not cause OCD in itself, it lowers a child's coping mechanisms.

In reality all behaviour is complex. It is best seen as being multi-modal – in other words several influences can be involved in producing a particular behaviour. An

161

inherited disposition to OCD may need certain environmental features, including stress, to trigger off the behaviour. It might also be that there are a number of ways by which a child can develop OCD.

It is interesting to note that similar types of OCD are shared by people from different countries and cultures. Rituals around entering and leaving rooms are common; so, too, are issues about cleanliness and infections. Similarly, another 'popular' behaviour is collecting and hoarding. These activities are reflected in the behaviour of many animals:

- cleanliness, etc. – grooming
- hoarding and gathering – nesting
- entering and leaving – settling.

It could well be that, for yet to be fully understood reasons, certain innate behavioural patterns that are programmed into us all are triggered in some children for some reason and are beyond the child's conscious control. This type of explanation, known as 'neuro-ethological', is held by many child psychiatrists (Rapoport, 1990).

A further and more recent development is the idea that some forms of OCD seem to be associated with such childhood illnesses as strep throat and viral infections. It seems that, if children who are genetically susceptible to OCD have a strep infection, this leads to a part of the brain associated with OCD being damaged. OCD consequently develops quickly. Where OCD is triggered by a strep infection it is called PANDAS – Paediatric Autoimmune Neuropsychiatric Disorders Associated with Strep. Not all medical professionals are aware of this development.

Does it really matter if a child has OCD?

As with many disorders it is easier to prevent something early from developing into a more serious problem than to cure it later. It is clear that children who are distracted by their thoughts or habits have less free emotional and mental energy to tackle the learning challenges they are presented with.

Additionally, school staff have a genuine commitment to the 'whole child', not just the targets the child achieves – children are much more than learning machines. We are, of course, equally concerned with their successful involvement with peers and their developing a positive sense of self-worth. A happy child is a happy learner.

It matters also in the long run, as the following quote from an adult sufferer to a child psychiatrist illustrates:

> Looking back, it seems that the hurt of an OCD attack was more psychologically painful than the death of my father, whom I loved. This may be very hard for a normal person such as yourself to comprehend. Nonetheless, it's sadly true. My sense of loss and grief was trivial and short-lived compared to any of the hundreds of OCD attacks I have had in my life.
>
> (Rapoport, 1990)

The child's point of view

The real number of children suffering with OCD is difficult to ascertain because of their reluctance to seek help either from parents or other adults for fear of being judged as either abnormal or personally responsible. They often feel that they are freaks and that their thoughts and behaviour are signs of their madness. They feel ashamed and embarrassed to tell family or friends how dominated and controlled they are by the OCD. Children who are trapped by OCD are sad, bewildered and troubled.

> My friends don't know that I have OCD. I keep it a secret because I'm afraid they will laugh at me.
>
> (child with OCD)

Helping children to understand that OCD is not their fault is very important.

Key points for children and young people

1   OCD is an illness for which you are not responsible.
2   Think of the thoughts as if they were 'junk mail'. You are being asked to open messages that you didn't want.
3   Give the OCD a nickname: 'Mr Clean Me', 'Mr Perfect' or 'Checking Man'. You are not the OCD.
4   Practise what you would like to say to OCD – 'I am too busy to listen to you' – and say it.
5   Keep remembering what it is you would like to be doing instead of the compulsive behaviour – maybe meeting friends. OCD wants to keep you doing its work rather than relaxing with your favourite book or listening to music.

6   Show who is boss – do it when you're ready. For example, if you have to perform a ritual, do it when you are ready, make it wait. You are in charge. Try to not do it perfectly. If it has to be done a set number of times, do slightly fewer times.

7   Keep reminding yourself of what you could be doing if you weren't indulging in the compulsive behaviour.

8   Keep a note of all those times when you do not have this problem. Look at what you were doing – where were you? Do those things that help you to avoid the compulsive behaviour more often.

9   Use the ten-minute rule. Resist performing the behaviour for ten minutes and, if after that time you still need to do it, then do it. Practise increasing the time that you resist doing it.

10 Get angry, get bossy with OCD; avoid feeling scared and trapped. The more you can change your feelings of helplessness, the better you will feel and the more able to take control of the OCD.

Parents

Parents can be unaware that a child is suffering with OCD. This can be due to a combination of the child's success in keeping it secret and the parents' not wishing to see it. The younger the child is, the more important and active the role of the family will be.

Parents will experience many emotions over OCD. Guilt, anger and fear are common. They know how to care for and support their child when they have a 'normal' illness – measles or a broken leg. But few know about OCD.

Key points for parents

1   OCD is a complex disorder and there is no simple explanation for why some children suffer from it and others do not.

2   OCD is nobody's fault. Focus on what you have done and will do successfully in bringing up your child.

3   Only share information about your child's OCD with those you trust.

4   Ask your child how he or she would like to be helped and supported.

5   Remember you are the executive – your child needs you to be in charge because he or she cannot control the OCD. Therefore taking a break and looking after yourself is essential if you are to give of your best. A stressed parent is not going to help things get better.

6 Keep focusing on your child's strengths and qualities. He or she is more than the OCD.

7 'Has' not 'is'. Your child *has* OCD – he or she is *not* 'an OCD child'.

8 Focus on your child's efforts and successes in increasing his or her control over the OCD, and give feedback.

9 Be flexible with your expectations, within a framework of consistency. Sometimes you will need to bend.

10 Take an active interest in other areas of your child's life, his or her hobbies, etc.

Assessment

How do I know if a child has OCD?

The most important question to ask when we are trying to decide whether or not a child is suffering from OCD is: 'Do the habits or thoughts get in the way of the child's academic or social life in school?' A thought or a habit indicates OCD if:

- the child cannot stop doing it
- it gets in the way of the child being like any other learner
- the child spends time and effort trying to stop it.

The four key elements of OCD

Use the following rating scale to decide whether a child may be suffering from OCD (from Rapoport, 1990) and score using Figure 1, p. 16:

1 How much time do the habits or thoughts take up?

0 none
1 less than an hour a day
2 severe: 1–3 hours per day
3 extreme constant intrusion

2 How much interference do the habits or thoughts represent within the child's normal school life?

0 none
1 mild

2   mild to moderate

3   moderate but manageable

4   extreme

3   *How much distress is being caused?*

0   none

1   mild, infrequent

2   moderate

3   severe anxiety observed

4   extreme, near constant distress

4   *How much effort is needed to resist the habits and thoughts?*

0   minimal resistance prevents the problem

1   some effort needed

2   a great deal of effort required

3   no matter how hard he or she tries, child usually fails

If the scores are 3 or 4 then there is a definite need to discuss concerns with the child's carers and consider referring to the school doctor

Common OCDs in children

Contamination

It is estimated that some 85% of children who suffer from OCD have some form of washing compulsion. Chansky (2000) provides a useful list of warning signs, some key ones of which are:

- long trips to the bathroom
- multiple and/or long showers
- excessive use of soap, towels, toilet paper
- avoidance of door handles, public toilets
- concerns about germs and illnesses
- avoidance of physical contact with others.

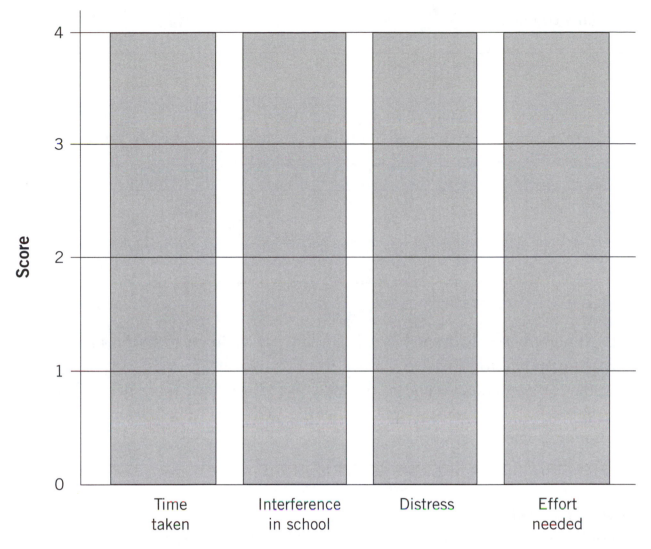

FIGURE 7.1 Scoring OCD: key elements

Iqbal

After a talk on AIDS Iqbal began to become obsessed with a fear that he would contract the disease. Everything he did, the way he walked, the clothes he wore, the food he ate, all contained a threat to him of catching AIDS. It destroyed his friendships and made his family life into a nightmare.

Checking compulsions

Ann

Ann was very competent at maths, but gradually her OCD led to her grades lowering. She seemed to need to check every answer two to five times on the calculator in case she had tapped in the wrong figures.

Rituals

Harry

Each night before bedtime Harry had a long set of rituals to go through. Each room had to be passed through in a certain way. His washing followed a strict set of guidelines and he had rules as to how many times he brushed each tooth. If he was interrupted the entire ritual had to be started from the beginning again.

Hoarding or collecting

Many children collect a range of objects, either believing that they will need them one day or that something bad will happen if they don't. Sometimes it just 'feels right' to pick things up. Steketee (1999) suggests that hoarding shows a cognitive blind spot. The child's thinking is dominated by the 'What if?' of needing the objects, which overruns the consequences of not throwing things away.

Hair pulling (trichotillomania)

Hair pulling is both similar to and different from OCD. They both demonstrate a compulsive aspect to certain behaviours and both respond to similar treatments. But whereas in OCD there is a reduction of tension through engaging in the behaviours, with hair pulling there is an enjoyable, appetitive dimension.

The possible causes of hair pulling are similar to those of OCD. Very young children may do it to reduce anxiety, while for adolescents it can be an over-learned grooming response. Whatever the cause, the difficulties and stress associated with it are self-evident. An adolescent may avoid many activities that would risk the exposure of their habit – swimming, roller coasters, dating, etc. The feeling of being different and the associated depression and lack of self-worth cannot be underestimated.

(The term 'trichotillomania' was first used in 1889 by a French doctor. *Trich* is the Greek word for 'hair' and *tillo* means 'to pull'. Mania is an abnormal love. Most hair pullers are female and this may be for social reasons. There may also be many male hair pullers, but it is much easier and more socially acceptable for a man to have little or no hair as compared with women.)

Whether the hair pulling is emotionally caused or whether it is mainly an over-learned habit, it does seem that the older the child is, the more he or she is able to develop more adaptive coping mechanisms. It is not uncommon for the cause of the original behaviour to have long disappeared and that it is now a response to increased stresses or boredom. Hair pullers frequently report being able to better control the habit the busier they are. But, like most complex behaviours, a range of interventions is usually required to overcome such over-ingrained behaviours. There are more self-help books available today, so that once the difficulty is out in the open there are proven ideas that can help a young person take charge and beat the habit (Keuthen *et al.*, 2001).

This is not an exclusive list of compulsive disorders. Children can create OCDs out of anything, from asking questions about the weather to coughing. Note how several will combine together – an obsession with cleanliness will often lead to a complex set of rituals.

A working model

Having explored common explanations for OCD it is important to draw some of these ideas together. This is more than a theoretical exercise. It can be extremely helpful for both the child and his or her carers to be able to make sense of what can be seen as bizarre or even insane behaviour.

Let us accept that there may well be a biological or inherited disposition to some children developing OCD. All children experience fears and anxieties as they grow and these can be coped with by developing certain behaviours that allow the negative emotional energy to be released. The behaviours distract the individual's system from the fears at hand, and the energy needed to carry out the behaviours dissipates the negative emotions.

Behaviours that serve such a function as allowing negative emotions to be avoided are self-rewarding. They are learned and, as they are performed more and more, they often become strongly ingrained patterns of behaviour – habits. This is OCD. The mind is scanning the world for potential threats and if any are perceived, whether real or imagined, then the anxiety-reducing behaviour is triggered off. Often the trigger can be boredom. When children are actively engaged in something they enjoy doing, the OCD is less evident.

Chansky (2000) uses the idea of 'junk mail' to illustrate the difficulties faced by the child with OCD. It is as if the child is forced to open junk mail – post that is rubbish and irrelevant. Healthy thoughts and behaviours do not cause distress; but the mind of the child with OCD has become over-tuned to catch and respond to unhealthy thoughts that can cause worry – I might get ill; my mum and dad might have an accident.

OBSESSION	DISTRESS	COMPULSION	RELIEF
fear of dirt	anxiety	hand washing	less anxiety

FIGURE 7.2 OCD profile

The obsession – the thought, fear of contamination or of being left or excluded – triggers off a *distress* anxiety response in the child (see Figure 7.2). Firstly because the thought has a self-contained fear element – being poisoned or left out, etc. is naturally scary. But there is another side as well, which is especially true as children become older: 'I am worrying about something for no good reason.' This in itself is worrying. Shakeela, for example, worried about walking off the pavement into oncoming traffic. But she also worried about having such irrational worries. To tell someone about her fears was impossible because she knew that other people did not share her fears.

The distress now triggers the compulsive thought or behaviour, which is the attempt somehow to reduce the negative feelings: 'I have to wash my hands often to reduce the risk of being infected.'

Boredom as an OCD trigger

OCD can be triggered by boredom. When the child or young person is not fully engaged in an activity there is a danger that the mind might start thinking anxiety-provoking thoughts. As a way of coping the child distracts himself or herself by carrying out the ritualistic behaviours which serve to allay the anxiety. Some children will control the OCD to a certain extent by trying to keep themselves busy. While this is a positive step, it does not go far enough. Unless they actively learn to relax and cope with moderate levels of anxiety when they are aware that their thoughts are irrational they will always be prey to the OCD. They cannot remain busy 24 hours a day.

School-based interventions

Children and young people who suffer from mild OCD have similar levels of intelligence to any other group of children. They are as bright or as in need of support as the next. *But* when they are in class and being internally distracted by mental images and thoughts that threaten them with anxiety then it is not surprising that they are unlikely to achieve their potential. Similarly, if they are being pushed into carrying out a range of ritualistic behaviours, they will not have the same amount of time and mental energy for their schoolwork and friends.

(Note: children and young people with severe forms of OCD will often be on medication as one aspect of a multifaceted programme of support.)

In school the areas of difficulty are many and, as we have seen, are commonly related to:

- hoarding
- cleanliness
- contamination
- need for perfection.

Because of the amount of time children spend in school it is often there that a child's difficulties are first noticed. School staff need to be aware that a learner with OCD is extremely vulnerable to low self-esteem; giving positive feedback on the child's strengths and qualities can help challenge this. There is also a danger of a child with OCD becoming socially isolated from peers, so classroom activities structured to include all are essential.

The effect of OCD on learning

OCD leads the learner to:

- have less free energy for thinking
- be distracted by the need to carry out ritualistic behaviour
- appear to be lazy and lack motivation
- have poor peer relationships.

Coping vs. challenging

As with most difficulties there are two sides to the support we can give. Coping means we accept the disorder and look for ways to minimise the negative effect of the symptoms, while challenging involves looking to remove the condition altogether.

Teaching the child coping skills

Here we can look at a number of appropriate strategies that minimise the effect of the OCD on the child or young person in school and help him or her to cope with the symptoms.

Perfectionism

A characteristic of all OCD symptoms is that they are time-consuming. Combined with the obsessional thought that unless work is completely perfect it should not be handed in, the stress on a child increases and, consequently, so does the power of the OCD. In order to reduce the stress the teacher should:

- set short assignments
- give clear time limits
- value mistakes as part of the learning process.

Cleanliness

Paradoxically, the freer children feel about being able to go to the toilet to wash their hands, the less strong is the need. When they are unsure if they will be allowed they will sit and anguish over whether to ask or not. To minimise the anxiety in the child it is advisable to:

- negotiate a reasonable number of 'free trips'

- remove the need for the learner to ask for permission
- enable the learner to monitor his or her own behaviour.

Handwriting

This is an area fraught with OCD opportunities. Perfectionist attitudes can emerge, as well as rigidity over the shape of letters, etc. In order to reduce the potential stress the teacher could:

- provide a laptop computer
- allow photocopying of other learners' work
- set agreed targets as to how much is needed.

A useful approach to consider is *solution-focused brief therapy*. This is based on the idea that, because no problem is perfect (in other words no problem occurs all the time), when the problem is not presenting itself is when the solution is taking place. Whenever children are not involved with their OCD we should look to see what they are doing. Who are they with? Because people are too busy analysing the problem they don't notice these possible solutions.

Change is inevitable, but gradual, and if people are looking for the 'big fix' – the solution that removes the problem completely – then they will wait a long time. What usually happens is that problems diminish little by little.

School staff can help learners to analyse those times when they seem not to have the problem and when are they able to cope marginally better.

1. Who were they with?
2. What activity were they doing?
3. What strategies did they use to control the problem behaviour?
4. Homework assignment: *Between now and next week notice all those examples of things getting better.* This simple approach can help all involved to notice signs of improvements rather than only seeing the problem.

Cognitive behavioural therapy

The two dominant strands of OCD are the behaviours and the thoughts. It is not surprising, then, that the two methods of intervention come from:

- Behavioural modification
- Cognitive therapy.

These two methods have of late combined to become one of the most active and effective therapies to exist. Presented below are some of the key interventions from each. When a school is able to provide some level of teacher or support assistant time, then some of these interventions can be chosen and implemented with confidence.

Behavioural interventions

Exposure with Response Prevention (ERP)

This approach works to help the child break the OCD down into small parts that can be systematically challenged. The logic behind the behavioural approach is elegant and simple: 'if something is repeated enough times with no significant consequence, it tends to lose its attention value' (Toates, 1990).

Obsessive thoughts that generate anxiety are never confronted, because the compulsive, irrational behaviours reduce the irrational fear. There is no real link between the thought and the outcome; for example, the fear held by the excessive hand washer of 'becoming sick through touching things' is never tested because he or she is washing his or her hands all the time. If the learned link can be broken between the obsessive thoughts and the compulsive behaviour then the child will be gaining control.

The fear thermometer

It is important to grade the level of fear that children are experiencing; this allows them to see progress being made. The child can see the grade before, during, and after he or she takes control (after Chansky, 2000).

Step 1

Help the child to grade different situations according to the amount of fear they might cause.

10 Get me out of here
 9
 8
 7
 6
 5 This is hard but I can cope

4

3

2

1 No problem

Step 2

Work out with the child or young person the type of things that he or she would put at 10, 5 and 1:

10 ....

5 ....

1 ....

Step 3

Teach relaxation skills – breath control
Say 'relax' as you breathe in deeply to the count of 1–2–3 through the nose. Now breathe out to the count of 1–2–3 through your mouth. The breath must fill the belly, not just the diaphragm.

Self-talk
Practise positive thinking: 'I can cope with this,' 'I have done this before,' 'This is tough, but I can manage.'

Muscle relaxation
Work through the body's muscles. Tense them, hold and then relax, noticing the difference each time you let the tension out.

Step 4

The child chooses level of fear that he or she would like to work on. For example, if he or she has a need to count to 200 when hand washing, the child should work to break this habit, perhaps by counting in fives, or only counting to

150. Always start at levels that can be managed successfully. Child records fear level.

Step 5

Present child with the fear situation; child practises relaxation and records score.

Step 6

After agreed time – five or ten minutes – fear level recorded.

These procedures enable the child to see the fear levels gradually reducing as he or she is breaking the previously held associations.

Score

The level of fear the child felt before trying new tactics, how he or she felt while doing it, and his or her fear level afterwards.

Before   *During*   *After*

This approach is based on the proven fact that you cannot be both tense and relaxed at the same time. Therefore, by choosing a manageable level of fear, its control can be broken by pairing it with a new and opposite emotional response, namely relaxation.

Habit reversal

This has proved to be an effective intervention for a range of OCDs, especially tics. It involves the child learning to behave in ways that are opposite to what the OCD requires. It is explained in the following steps.

Awareness training

Children are helped to see the specific components of their problem behaviour and the usual places where it occurs. They perform and describe these behaviours. Sometimes observing themselves in a mirror can be helpful.

Competing response training

Children are taught a new behaviour, which is incompatible with the OCD. For example, if the OCD causes them to screw their eyes up then they would be taught to focus on an object they like and look for a fixed time without blinking.

This skill would be practised daily and performed immediately after the tic occurred and just before one is likely to occur.

Motivation

This involves reviewing the inconvenience and the negative implications of the behavioural tic; these may include being stared at, being thought to be different, other children feeling nervous or frightened by the behaviour because they do not understand it.

Cognitive interventions

These involve children being able to express their inner thoughts. These will only apply if they are cognitively able to discuss their thoughts. Younger children will be less able to bring to conscious awareness some of the thoughts and beliefs that underpin their behaviours.

Thought stopping

'… stop … think … go …'

Children learn to say 'stop' to themselves when they feel the tic coming on. They then think of something they want to do to distract themselves. They decide how they will do it and then go and do it.

Thought checking

Because everyone's thinking can be irrational at times it is helpful to teach young people ways of checking the validity of what is going on in their minds by asking themselves the following questions:

1 What evidence is there to support what I am thinking?
2 What evidence is there against it?
3 If one of my best friends or a teacher I like knew what I was thinking, what would he or she say?
4 What would I say to my best friend if she had this thought?

Automatic thoughts

Too often our behaviour and feelings are triggered by our internal thoughts, and these can often be negative, such as 'I will fail in this situation' or 'I will be laughed at by my friends.' Through practice we can learn to trigger off positive internal thoughts instead, such as 'This is new but I can learn to be successful' or 'I have learned other skills before, so I will learn this one as well.'

Positive thoughts

- How I see myself: I am someone who can learn new skills.
- What I like about myself: I am determined to succeed.
- Good things I will do in the future: I will take control of what I think and what I do.

And finally – a shared humanity

At the heart of this chapter is the belief that children and young people who experience mild OCD are only different by degree from others. We all share a common humanity. We all have some degree of OCD. Understanding the nature of OCD enables school staff to develop, in partnership with a young person's family, interventions that can prevent a mild challenge from becoming more severe and debilitating.

Further reading

References

Adams, P. (1973) quoted in P. Thomsen (2001) *From Thoughts to Obsessions*, p. 97. London: Jessica Kingsley Publishers.

Chansky, T. (2000) *Free Your Child from Obsessive Compulsive Disorder*. New York: Crown Publishers.

Kendall, P. (2000) *Childhood Disorders*. Hove: Psychology Press.

Keuthen, N., Stein, D. and Christenson, G. (2001) *Help for Hair Pullers*. Oakland: New Harbinger Publications, Inc.

Rapoport, J. (1990) *The Boy Who Couldn't Stop Washing*. Glasgow: HarperCollins Publishers.

Rettew, D. (1992) cited by Chansky, T. (2000) *Free Your Child from Obsessive Compulsive Disorder*. New York: Crown Publishers.

Steketee, G. (1990) *Overcoming Obsessive-Compulsive Disorder*. Oakland: New Harbinger Publications, Inc.

Thomsen, P. (2001) *From Thoughts to Obsessions*. London: Jessica Kingsley Publishers.

Recommended reading

Graham, P. (2002) *Cognitive Behaviour Therapy for Children and Families*. Cambridge: Cambridge University Press.

Martin, G. and Pear, J. (1999) *Behaviour Modification*. New Jersey: Prentice Hall.

Selekman, M. (1993) *Pathways to Change*. New York: The Guilford Press.

Stallard, P. (2002) *Think Good – Feel Good*. Chichester: John Wiley and Sons Ltd.

Toates, F. (1990) *Obsessive Compulsive Disorder*. Kent: Thorsons.

Working with Groups

Introduction

Kim is six years old and has one-to-one support due to her aggressive behaviour. The teaching assistant in Kim's class reports that she is a pleasure to work with and that, when she is on her own, Kim is polite and co-operative. But when she is with her peers Kim is pushy and aggressive unless she is getting her own way.

It is not uncommon for children who face emotional and behavioural difficulties to behave well in a one-to-one situation with an adult. It is when they are in a group with their peers that their behaviour deteriorates dramatically. More and more today we refer to the difficulties of such children as being social, emotional and behavioural, rather than just emotional and behavioural. Yet, while most of us work with children in groups, little formal training in the understanding of group dynamics is provided. The more we understand the nature, purpose and function of groups then the better equipped we will be to support children who find such skills as turn-taking and sharing difficult to master or achieve.

In this chapter we will:

- define key terms
- consider the importance of groups
- explore why groups are difficult for children with social, emotional and behavioural difficulties.

What is a group?

While there is no hard and firm definition of what constitutes a group the following features are central. A group comprises members who:

- relate to each other
- can influence each other
- have an identity
- communicate with each other

● have some form of hierarchy.

This leads us to the next key term:

Group dynamics

When social psychologists were beginning to study groups, a key figure was Kurt Lewin who was carrying out research in the 1930s. He emphasised that groups are dynamic in that their members influence each other. Groups give identity to members and can pressure them to conform. Since Lewin's time our understanding of group dynamics has increased significantly. In fact, to many people, all psychology is essentially group psychology as that is where we live our lives – in a range of different groups. This includes the family as well as the class in school that a child belongs to.

What purpose do groups serve for young people?

We are all social animals. When we were children we depended on our carers to survive. Our personal identity is developed through our relationship to others, both within our family and outside. For example, I am a husband to a wife, a father to children, a son to a mother, a colleague at work. We are never without any links to one or other group.

As human beings we have many needs. We all need food, shelter and warmth. But after these basic needs are met other needs emerge that relate to social groups. Groups provide us with the following three core human needs:

1   The need to belong: being positively attached to other people
2   The need for power: influencing the goals and actions of others
3   The need for success: the enhancement of self-worth through achieving socially valued goals.

When these three needs coexist in a positive way then pupils will be ideal learners. Learners can enjoy belonging to their class, value the projects they are working on and enjoy the success of achieving set goals. These emotional needs are instrumental in driving pupils' behaviour and lead them to take up those roles within the group that help them meet their needs (see Figure 8.1).

EMOTIONAL NEED	BEHAVIOUR	ROLE WITHIN GROUP
approval	disruptive	class clown
care	passive	class mascot

FIGURE 8.1 Group roles

Awareness of these driving needs helps us to appreciate why we can only ever understand a child's behaviour if we look at the social context in which it takes place. To look at the child in isolation is to look at only half the answer. A pupil's behaviour is seeking to meet an emotional need within a group context. This leads us on to the third key question.

Why do so many children find it difficult to behave appropriately within class?

This is not a simple question – classroom behaviour is very complex and there are many interrelating factors that need to be understood to make sense of it. (If we fully understood it, then managing challenging behaviour in our classrooms would not be the problem that it clearly is in most schools.)

Some key factors

Ideally, before they even start attending school, most children learn a number of social skills at home within the family group that match school expectations:

- how to behave as a group member
- how to gain attention
- which emotions it is OK to express
- how to resolve conflicts in socially acceptable ways
- how to negotiate and compromise.

Some of us may remember when schools used 'traditional' methods for teaching – pupils sat in rows of desks and the teacher was at the front imparting knowledge. In those days everything was much calmer than it is today. Many factors contributed to this, including:

- learners were expected to be more passive recipients of knowledge, therefore there were less interactions between learners and teacher

- teachers were perceived as being in charge and had higher status
- children and parents were socialised to accept unquestioningly what schools did
- education was valued as a means of offering work opportunities, therefore parents were supportive of its importance.

As schools have moved towards more co-operative and collaborative learning methods, however, more and more children face difficulties and exhibit challenging behaviour. Davinder, for example, finds doing project work with his classmates very difficult. He becomes frustrated when they give him tasks to do that he doesn't like and fails to understand why he should listen to the ideas of others who at times don't agree with his suggestions.

Why is this? A plausible explanation is that children enter school with fewer of the basic social skills necessary to engage in active learning. The changing pattern of children's games and the growing use of the media and computer games naturally reduce the opportunities for some children to learn social skills.

For those children whose home background helps develop such skills as listening and sharing, then school life is an extension of their family life and they are more likely to have the will to succeed. These children are used to listening to the ideas of others and then having their views asked for and respected. They have come to expect people to justify their views, as well as being prepared to compromise when differences occur. Such experiences are invaluable for today's classrooms.

If a child has some degree of learning difficulty this will compound his or her lack of social skills. In many schools, especially secondary schools, children who find learning difficult have turned the school culture and ethos on its head. They have made failure seem like success and they name-call those children who engage positively with school ('boffins' and 'swots'). It is understandable that children who expect to fail will seek to protect their self-esteem. To this end the social, emotional and behavioural difficulties that many children show in certain lessons and with specific adults can be seen as an attempt by the child to avoid failure.

For some children who enter school with low self-esteem and poor learning experiences, groups, particularly classroom groups, are extremely threatening places. The goals that adults set up for the group are goals that they realise they cannot succeed in, such as being expected to plan work together, to take on different roles and to defer immediate satisfaction of what they would like to do. If they could have some success within the group they would achieve a sense of personal power. It would also mean that they were pursuing goals set down by school, which would help to give them a sense of belonging to a community with shared values. Because of their low expectation to succeed many children develop alternative goals such as:

- to challenge adult authority
- to undermine the curriculum aims.

Developmental factors

In younger children a sense of personal identity is influenced and shaped by such key people as parents and school staff. The younger the children are the more they see themselves 'through the eyes of significant others'. They are more concerned about how adults, rather than their peers, think and feel about them. But as they grow older it is their peers who take on an increasingly important role. During adolescence it is the reactions of their peers that come to matter as much, and often more, than those of adults. The influence that parents have diminishes. This can help explain why it is in secondary schools that classroom behaviour becomes such an issue. Adolescents are placed in groups – usually with peers of both gender. The values and attitudes of the group now influence the behaviour of individuals. Being challenging towards adults can increase a young person's status within the group. The adult may punish the adolescent but the perception of the individual and the group is that he or she is asserting his or her autonomy.

Theory to practice – mistaken goal analysis

The question now is how we can use our awareness of group behaviour to help us understand and support those children who find it difficult to participate positively in class. If we agree that the emotional needs of children are the main drive for inappropriate behaviour we can begin to develop models that can help us intervene in a more focused manner.

Group roles

If pupils misbehave, either through excessive disruptive behaviour or through hurting another child, then they should face the consequences. However, if they belong to the minority who do not respond to negative consequences (punishments), this suggests that their behaviour is being maintained by other factors, that is internal needs that they have learned to fulfil in ways that are not acceptable in the classroom. Whereas most children learn through positive discipline how to get attention appropriately, some only receive negative attention and punishment now becomes 'positive feedback' as it is the only attention they receive.

The following model, called 'mistaken goal analysis', was developed by Dreikurs, Grunwald and Pepper (1998). It was based on the work of Alfred Adler (1957), a one-time follower of Freud who broke away. Adler believed that the main drive for all people is their need to belong. As most children with social, emotional and behavioural difficulties tend to act out (that is their difficulties are observable and are intended to have an impact on other people) more in a group context than when alone or in one-to-one situations, this model certainly seems to have some face validity for an understanding of the behaviour problems that arise in group contexts.

Mistaken goal analysis

Dreikurs *et al.* (1998) set out the four main goals, one or more of which seem to be found in children who present behaviour problems in the classroom. These are:

- attention
- power
- revenge
- nurture.

Most children develop positive ways of belonging to the group/class through making friends, sharing and co-operating. By 'mistaken goals' Dreikurs *et al.* suggest that some children develop unconscious goals that reflect their own real or imagined experiences, determining how they behave when in a group.

Attention

Children who fail to obtain a valued place in the group can come to strive for attention at any cost. Consequently, even though the attention they receive may be negative – for example the teacher feels annoyed at the child for shouting out and sanctions him – this is negative attention which satisfies the child's need for some form of attention. The child may show off with peers and receive negative feedback – for example not being chosen to join in. While the child's behaviour is not satisfying his need to belong, he is nonetheless trying to relate to both adults and his peers.

Power

The child who strives for power is confrontational and determined to win at any cost. Adults who take the child on find that she will always come back with some attempt to dominate. Karen, for example, has been told to return to her seat by her teacher. As she does so she mutters a negative comment which is barely audible but loud enough for the teacher to ask her what she has said. Karen replies, 'Nothing that concerns you.' Such children often suffer from a sense of inferiority, perhaps because their own views and attempts to control events in their lives have been over-dominated by others stronger than them, and this pushes them on to more and more extreme ways to 'get their own way'.

Revenge

Some children develop a strong sense of injustice and can believe that they have been hurt or wronged in some way. These children will behave in hurtful and spiteful ways towards both other children and adults, for example by spoiling a friend's work or using obscene language that they detect upsets the adults. It is as if they are saying, 'I've been hurt, so you feel some of the pain that I've felt.' Children who hurt others are usually hurting inside themselves.

Nurture

The child who seeks nurture is the typically passive child. Such children can feel that the challenges in the classroom are beyond them and they try to draw adults in to parent them. Tim, for example, will sit and sulk when given a new task and wait for an assistant to offer him help. These children are rarely disruptive to others, but find it hard to engage with new challenges.

This model asks us to see children's behaviour as another form of communication which is telling us something about their needs. The trouble is usually that busy adults take the behaviour at its surface level. If we look behind it we can find clues to what the child really needs and this can inform any support programme we wish to put in place.

Figure 8.2 is a problem-solving model. Before we can decide which interventions to put in place, we need to generate a 'plausible hypothesis' about which of the mistaken goals we think the child is pursuing within the group context.

186

STEP 1	Describe the behaviour fully and clearly as you see it. Make sure that your descriptions are objective. The term 'aggressive behaviour' could be interpreted in different ways, but describing how one pupil hit another on the shoulder is clear and observable.
STEP 2	Personal reflex – record how the child's behaviour typically makes you feel (see Figure 8.3).
STEP 3	Response reflex – record how the child usually responds to your attempts to reprimand him (see Figure 8.3).
STEP 4	Recognition reflex – when you put your idea to the child (in a caring way) as to why he behaves as he does, do you notice any tell-tale nonverbal responses (eyes look away, blushing, fidgeting, etc.) (see Figure 8.3)?
STEP 5	Choose interventions to respond to the child's behaviour in a way which will help the child to get his needs met more appropriately (see Figure 8.4).

FIGURE 8.2 Data collection

Having obtained a plausible hypothesis as to what the child's behaviour is achieving for him or her, Figure 8.4 suggests interventions which will help to:

- redirect the behaviour in a positive direction
- teach the child how to get his or her needs met in more appropriate ways.

There are many other plausible explanations for behavioural difficulties in learners. Below is a list of useful questions that can help us to decide which explanation to pursue, including the goals we have already considered.

Indicative questions

1 Does the behaviour occur when new learning tasks are set?
   YES: plausible hypothesis – learning difficulties.

2 Does the behaviour occur during free and unstructured times?
   YES: plausible hypothesis – poor social skills.

3 Is the behaviour confrontational towards adults?
   YES: plausible hypothesis – need for power.

187

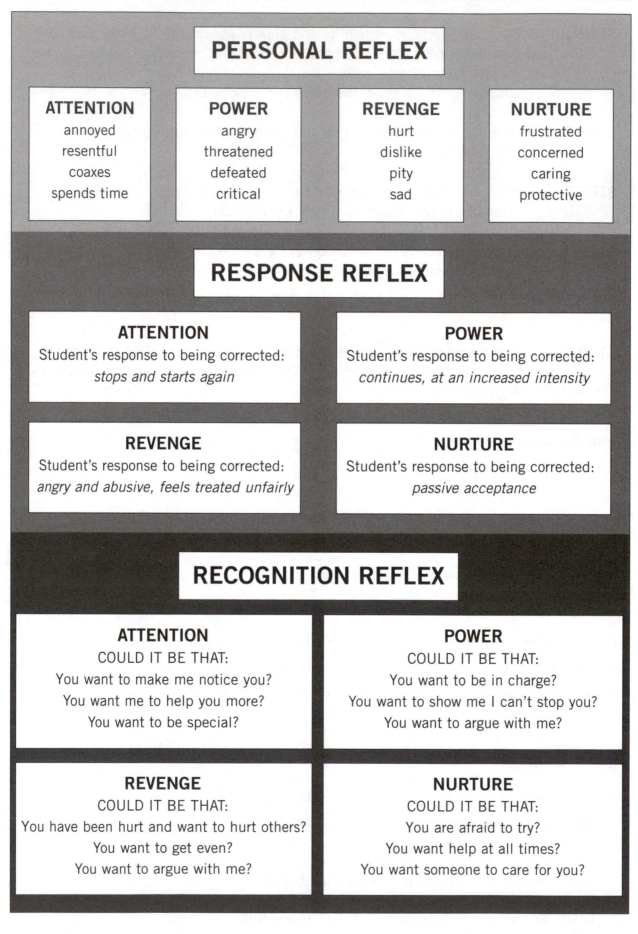

FIGURE 8.3 The three reflexes

Mistaken goal: plausible hypothesis	How to redirect student
POWER pupil is defiant and confrontational	• give responsibility/tasks • develop areas of strength • teach impulse-control skills • practise carrying out requests
REVENGE pupil often hurts or spoils work	• enhance self-esteem • set safety boundaries • develop empathy skills • teach ways of expressing feelings
NURTURE pupil is dependent on others	• promote independence • practise positive thinking • give choices • value contribution
ATTENTION pupil seeks adult time	• give attention when appropriate • use payback scheme • sit with role model • value contributions

FIGURE 8.4 Interventions for mistaken goals

4   Is the behaviour annoying towards adults?
    YES: plausible hypothesis – attention seeking.

5   Is the behaviour hurtful towards adults or other pupils?
    YES: plausible hypothesis – revenge.

6   Is the behaviour passive and dependent?
    YES: plausible hypothesis – need for nurture.

7   Has the child experienced any recent traumas?
    YES: plausible hypothesis – stress.

8   Does the pupil avoid mixing with peers?
    YES: plausible hypothesis – bullying/friendship difficulties.

9   Does the pupil respond negatively to specific adults?
    YES: plausible hypothesis – personality clash.

10 Has the pupil recently experienced loss or separation?
    YES: plausible hypothesis – bereavement.

Group behaviour

This problem-solving model can also help us understand the different roles that pupils take on in class. We are all familiar with such characters as: the bully, who dominates and forces his will on others; the class clown, who turns situations into being funny and entertaining to obtain attention; the victim, who seems to provoke others to treat her negatively; the leader, who has high status and helps the group achieve valued goals, for example in sport; and the class mascot, who is liked and protected by others and often is or acts younger than his peers and therefore needs some form of protection. It is reasonable to expect that the roles that children take up within a group reflect their internal emotional needs.

Using Figure 8.5 it is possible to see which roles dominate for any particular child. The typical behaviours that are associated with particular needs are grouped with those roles that usually enable these mistaken needs to be obtained. If you use such a grid for any particular pupil you will find that, while you do place some ticks everywhere, there will be a preponderance of ticks around a particular need. This will enable you either to discuss this with the pupil or to implement an intervention plan based on your analysis. To use the grid focus on the behaviours that you observe in a student and then see which role best fits the description.

Classroom subgroups

Managing a large class is no easy achievement and doing so successfully demonstrates the true skill of the teacher. Trying to understand and meet the needs of 30 pupils would test anyone. A useful approach is to break the class down into subgroups, each of which have different needs to the others. There are two such models worth considering.

Model 1   The OK groups

Peter Galvin (1999) suggests that there are four main subgroups in a difficult-to-manage class. In Figure 8.6 you can see each of these subgroups identified and the key task for any classroom manager.

ROLE														BEHAVIOUR
POWER	• challenger	• dominator	• defier	• bully	**BELONGING**	• comedian	• victim/loner	• mascot	• attention seeker	**GOALS**	• rebel	• cynic	• saboteur	• loser	
															Refuses requests
															Answers back
															Verbally aggressive
															Physically aggressive
															Has few friends
															Fools around
															Follows the crowd
															Petty interruptions
															Lacks motivation
															Disaffected
															Avoids new challenges
															No homework/equipment

FIGURE 8.5 Functional analysis of behaviour and roles

Subgroup 1. The very OK

The top five. These are the pupils who nearly always behave well. Because of this they are often passed over. They need feedback, an occasional but regular good word about how much they are valued.

Subgroup 2. The average OK

Around 15. These are the pupils who are little trouble, the 'run-of-the-mill' kids as Galvin refers to them. They will finish their school career with, 'Thanks, I'm off'. They need to be motivated and involved.

Subgroup 3. The not very OK

About eight. These are the pupils that we cannot ignore. They are constantly needing guidance, reminders, reprimands and sanctions and seem to thrive on disrupting any lesson. They have to be managed.

Subgroup 4. The desperately not OK

Around two. These are the pupils who are either statemented for their special needs or you wish they were. They usually display difficult behaviours in a wide range of different contexts, both structured and unstructured. You are usually aware of their background and they are pupils who have probably faced a number of out-of-school at-risk factors.

FIGURE 8.6 Model 1 – the OK groups

If you are faced with a difficult class Galvin suggests that the subgroup that will pay immediate dividends is subgroup 3. These are the students you cannot ignore, therefore the sooner you get to know them the more effective your management strategies can be.

Model 2   Motivation, expectancy and effort

The effort that pupils make in any lesson can be summed up by the following equation:

$$effort = f (expectancy/value)$$

That is to say, effort depends on pupils' expectations to succeed and the value they place on what they are learning. This model can help us break a class down into four subgroups. See Figure 8.7.

Subgroup A. The engaged
Pupils who expect to succeed and value the curriculum are our ideal pupils. They engage willingly in our lessons.

Subgroup B. The avoiders
Pupils who know they could manage the work, but don't see the point or the value of it, will do as little as possible.

Subgroup C. Those needing protection
Pupils who value the work you set them but do not believe they can cope with it will seek to protect their fragile self-esteem. These are the pupils who answer 'yes' when you ask if they have understood your instructions. You might know that they will not be able to do the work without some form of support.

Subgroup D. The rejectors
These are the pupils who are at risk of truanting. They neither value the curriculum nor have any expectation to succeed if they tried.

FIGURE 8.7 Model 2 – motivation, expectancy and effort

By looking at a class through model 2 you can see that the different behaviours you observe can be explained in different terms. Each group will benefit from focused support as they each have different reasons for not working in the class.

Some ideas as to how we might support each of the subgroups in model 2 are presented in Figure 8.8.

Subgroup A. The engaged
As this group is engaged there is no need for interventions.

Subgroup B. The avoiders
- involve interests – can their hobbies and interests be used in their learning?
- cost–benefit analysis – what will be the students' gains for trying harder?
- analyse long-term goals – do the students have long-term goals that can be related to their present situation?
- alternative curriculum – are there any alternative, work-related courses that they could join?

Subgroup C. Those needing protection
- learning support – is there a learning mentor available to work with them?
- record successes – can their short-term successes be highlighted?
- differentiate learning goals – make sure targets set match their current abilities
- small group work – can they work with supportive peers?

Subgroup D. The rejectors
- home–school links – actively contact and involve parents/carers
- counselling – make one-to-one time available to explore issues
- goal-setting – involve students in setting realistic goals
- combine strategies for subgroups B and C that are appropriate (this is because all behaviour has a mixture of different motives and is rarely explained simply by one factor).

FIGURE 8.8 Interventions for model 2

When you use either of these models be sure to write the actual names of the pupils under each heading. This can be used as a reminder to you as to the type of intervention that is most likely to be effective with each student or group.

Group skills

The 'problem' behaviour in class of many children is a reflection of their lack of the core skills needed to function successfully in today's classrooms. The increased emphasis on learning in groups, of learning being a social activity, is a huge change from traditional methods. More and more schools are recognising that some children misbehave not because they are unwilling to conform but because they are unable to conform. They lack the core skills. And when this combines with low expectations to succeed through a history of learning difficulties then it is hardly surprising that their frustrations lead them to behave inappropriately. Using the core group skills profile presented below you will be able to see where the areas of weakness are for a particular pupil.

A score of three or less in any category indicates that this is an area for development. Above three shows a functional level of competency.

If a pupil lacks those core skills that are essential for successful group work then positive action needs to be taken to ensure positive progress. Even the most effective sanction will not teach a pupil how to do what she currently cannot do.

Scaffolding

A helpful term when constructing an individual support programme is 'scaffolding'. For Vygotsky (1962) learning is a social process. Children learn from those they interact with – peers and adults. Scaffolding is the process by which the next step in the learning process is modelled or cued. The process of scaffolding also occurs with behaviour. Children who have not experienced adults modelling trust, care, listening, etc. sufficiently for them to have learnt these social skills will require scaffolding to enable them to move from their existing limited skills to new skills appropriate for success in group work.

Imran

Imran (eight years old) seemed able to cope when in a small group of two or three. At such times he seemed to relate well with his peers, sharing toys and being generally co-operative. However, during playtimes when there were many more children around he seemed to forget all these skills. He would run around the playground bumping into other children and seemed unable to play organised games such as football.

Scaffolding techniques

1   Observation. With an adult, Imran observed the games other children were playing and discussed what was happening.
2   Role differentiation. Using role play, Imran played games which involved him behaving differently in different situations.
3   Buddying. Several other children were involved in supporting Imran for short periods of playtimes, during which Imran was actively encouraged to take part in a football game – sometimes being the goalkeeper, sometimes striker.

Outcome

After a four-week period Imran was securely involved in the organised games during playtimes and was a lot more confident in himself.

Core group skills profile

Student's name: ....

Completed by: ....

Date: ....

Circle the number in the one column which best describes the student.

	Rarely	Sometimes	Often	Always
Social Competence				
1 Gets on well with peers	0	1	2	3
2 Mixes appropriately with strangers	0	1	2	3
3 Can express needs to range of adults	0	1	2	3
4 Behaves well in school	0	1	2	3
5 Relates well with other family members	0	1	2	3

SCORE   /15

	Rarely	Sometimes	Often	Always
Personal Interaction Skills				
6 Uses eye contact appropriately	0	1	2	3
7 Contributes to conversations	0	1	2	3
8 Aware of verbal and nonverbal cues	0	1	2	3
9 Can empathise with others	0	1	2	3
10 Can give and accept compliments	0	1	2	3

SCORE   /15

	Rarely	Sometimes	Often	Always
Social Problem-solving				
11 Deals with unfair criticism	0	1	2	3
12 Can think of a range of solutions	0	1	2	3
13 Can make new friends	0	1	2	3
14 Manages conflicts positively	0	1	2	3
15 Deals with teasing effectively	0	1	2	3

SCORE   /15

Scaffolding principle

In devising a programme to help students develop the necessary social skills we need to analyse their current skill levels in a specific context. To achieve this the following questions need to be considered.

1 What can they do now?
2 What can they do with support?
3 What do I need to do to help them?

Managing difficult groups

'The elephant in the kitchen' syndrome

When we are confronted by difficult or unpleasant situations there is a normal tendency in all of us to avoid truths that can be painful. Imagine a family which has a huge elephant in the kitchen. Everybody squeezes around it, but no one will ask the question, 'What is that elephant doing in the kitchen?' for fear of breaking the family secret. This can be the same with difficult groups – the painful truth is avoided. Jasmine, for example, is being bullied by a number of girls in her class. All the other members of the class know that this is going on, but no one will talk about it. Her class teacher is aware that things are not right but doesn't know why. The shock tactic of bringing the secret into the open, however, can often be the first step in going forward. Children, like adults, are used to looking the other way. Show your determination to improve relationships, teaching and learning.

Below are some principles and techniques worth bearing in mind when you are dealing with a difficult group.

1 Stranger in the room. Visitors can create new dynamics that can positively affect pupils' behaviour. You might, for example, invite into the classroom a colleague, a parent or students from another class doing some observations.
2 Shock tactics. Put aside your lesson plan and, in a caring way, challenge the group to look at the difficulties that are preventing you teaching and them learning.
3 Self-esteem activities. Develop a wide range of ways to show that there are positive consequences for appropriate behaviour. Such rewards could be a special video, visit or a student-chosen activity.
4 Letters home for positive reasons. Be ready to send notes home commenting on improvements, contributions, effort, etc. Pupils in difficult groups need encouragement to risk changing.

General guidelines

Always treat difficult groups with respect and avoid talking down to them. Show through your behaviour that you are determined to be consistent and fair.

The quicker you can establish routines the better it will be. Spend time establishing how students come into your room, how equipment is distributed, how homework is set and collected and how latecomers are dealt with. If getting specific equipment ready disrupts your teaching, establish a routine to deal with it.

You can have the greatest impact when you begin to teach a new group. The students probably don't yet know each other and this is when you can establish your expectations. If you do not a group culture will develop, which might be negative.

Rewards, responsibilities and self-esteem

Keep a log book of students' good behaviour, achievements, etc. At the end of each week read out their successes. Your intention is to break any well-established routines of members of the group defining themselves through their problem behaviour.

Have a reward system so that you can quickly and quietly give positive feedback on behaviour or work that you like (for example sticky dots). Reward students when they have completed even simple jobs. Set lots of easy (but realistic) tasks to ensure success. Send pupils to other members of staff to show their work.

Make a point of turning problem behaviours into ways of increasing students' personal responsibility. Make sure that they understand that it is their behaviour that determines either the rewards or punishments that they receive. They are responsible for their behaviour and your intention should be to help them take this responsibility and make the best choices.

Rules, routines and sanctions

Always start lessons in a set, organised way. Make sure you give your attention to those who are carrying out your instructions appropriately.

The more that pupils are involved in making the rules then the easier it will be for you to enforce them on their behalf. If you establish that they each have a right to learn, that others have the same right and that you have the right to teach then any disruption can be dealt with now as violating a basic ground rule of the group.

React quietly to any individual who is causing disruption. Remind her of your expectation and leave her with a 'Return to your seat, thank you'. This conveys an expectation that the individual will carry out your request. Remember that many adolescents, especially, view 'hard requests' as threats to their freedom (a core aspiration) and respond with increased defiance. 'Return to your seat' can be seen as an open invitation to a power struggle and a defiant response of 'make me'. While 'Return to your seat, thank you', with the adult turning away from the student, allows the student to do as asked but when she is ready, thus 'saving face'.

Don't make an issue out of low-level disruption but make sure the pupils know your procedure for dealing with challenging behaviour. Increase the sanction if the pupil begins to disrupt others or you.

Always follow through on sanctions. To the pupil it is the certainty that something will happen rather than the size of the consequence that is effective.

Grouping

Be decisive about seating in your room and change seating regularly. When you allow students to sit with friends make sure it is conditional upon them working effectively.

Encourage students to co-operate with each other by using team points in the form of marks out of ten for group work, to be given to the group as a whole. At the end of the week allocate rewards negotiated with the class, such as choosing activities, if teams have earned at least 50% of their potential score.

Activities, tasks and targets

Use short, timed tasks to build up to more detailed or difficult work. Breaking projects down ensures that at the end of a lesson each pupil can have a sense of achievement. One way to do this is to set five different tasks on different tables. Individuals or groups do as much as they can in ten minutes and then move on.

> *Remember*: set (short) task, give feedback, set task, give feedback, etc.

The group leader

Whether you are the leader of the class or of a small group it is you who are in charge. Knowledge of the group will also allow you to spot the leaders within groups. Working with these leaders will have a ripple effect, in that if you influence such key people in the group they will influence others who look to them for approval. Remember that young people look to their peers as their key reference group – we should make use of this knowledge.

Your aim is to remove those barriers that prevent children engaging with the learning experience that you have planned for them. We have seen that there are many reasons why some children try to avoid engaging with work in groups. It is, therefore, all the more important when a group is being established that you ensure that the correct group norms are stressed. It might be that you take some key norms from your school's behaviour policy. For example these might be:

● the right to learn
● the right to be safe
● the right to be valued.

These could be used as a starting point. You can then discuss what these mean within your class or group. Frequent reminders of these rules will be essential for those groups whose behaviour can be challenging. By adding some rules that are unique to your group you will encourage a sense of belonging, identity and ownership.

Remember that when your group has established their rights they need also to consider their responsibilities, namely:

● to enable others to learn
● to help others to feel safe
● to value others
● to respect the opinions of others.

Developing group identity

Helping a class develop a sense of belonging is a very important process. The pupils we are talking about here are each struggling, sometimes fighting, for a position in the group. While a classroom is not the jungle (it just feels like that sometimes) we should not ignore some basic principles of group psychology. Classrooms cause tensions – the need to be an individual versus the need to be a group member.

You might like to try the following activity on your pupils – and yourself. Ask students if they can write down ten different answers to the question:

'Who am I?'

If you collect their answers you will find that some fall under one or other of these two headings:

1 *Collectivistic qualities* – the answer shows the student's awareness of self in relationship to others, e.g. 'I am a student', 'I am a boy/girl'.
2 *Individualistic qualities* – the answer reflects personal traits, habits or interests, e.g. 'I am a football fan', 'I am a happy person'.

Is your group made up of individuals who define themselves more in collectivistic terms or individualistic terms? While there are no right or wrong answers the traits that each individual brings can make a group identity easier or harder to achieve. If there is a predominance of individualistic traits within the group then there is a definite need to develop some collectivistic qualities to avoid the group being over-competitive:

Individualistic	Collectivistic
personal goals	shared goals
competitive	co-operative

The more positive an identity pupils can have towards their group then the more confident and positive they will be towards the tasks set them. Ideally each pupil would:

● value his/her own contribution to the group
● be proud to be part of the group
● believe that others rate the group positively.

Achieving group identity – some ideas

1 Develop group structure, that is have a range of classroom responsibilities that all members must at some time fulfil, for example taking on the role of paper/display board monitor.
2 Give feedback to the group from other high-status individuals, such as the head or a deputy head teacher, as to how much progress they are seen to be making.

3   Give feedback on results of group effort, such as by displaying work in class or around school.

4   Set targets and rewards that can be achieved only through each member contributing within the group, for example, someone records a project, another produces models and a third makes a quiz or word search to use when the project is being presented to others.

5   Develop routines and rituals for recognising group success, for example the theme song of the local football team could be played on special occasions.

6   Develop a group record that allows individuals to record successes. This should include objective, methods used, date complete and comments on the outcome.

7   Make a photographic record of the group's activities, either to be kept in a file or displayed on the class wall.

8   Develop a routine for saying goodbye to any class members when they leave, for whatever reason, for example with a card completed by all members of the group, and ways of welcoming new members, such as sharing group experiences and memories and pairing the new member up with a buddy.

9   Develop a class motto, for example by putting the group's own words to the theme song of the local football team.

10 Join with the group in extracurricular activities such as sport or music.

Remember the norm of reciprocity – 'you get what you give'. The more positive and determined you are for the group to succeed the more likely you are to receive help from them in your goal. Aggressive and punitive control techniques, such as shouting and using threats, produce the same responses (aggressive behaviours and a non-co-operative attitude) in students.

Leaders' qualities, skills and attitude

There are many personal qualities and skills that combine to make a leader either effective or not. The four key behavioural techniques that require further consideration are as follows:

1   Nonverbal behaviour.
2   Creating a plan of action – trial and error learning.
3   Accentuating the positive.
4   Personal resiliency.

A complex system will only change when individuals are prepared to tackle the problems they face. When you become aware of a problem with a group it becomes an opportunity for you to improve the group. If you ignore it, it will not get better. Children with social, emotional and behavioural difficulties have more respect for school staff who try to improve matters than those who just accept them.

1. Nonverbal behaviour

While we may be conscious of the content of what we are saying, the real impact comes from the way we say it. Being mindful of our body language can help us project a confident and assertive message when managing groups of children. Voice control is also an aspect of nonverbal communication. We can convey enthusiasm, determination and concern by the slightest change in voice tone.

2. Plan of action

Use the framework below to set up a mini project systematically.

Step 1 – identify and describe
What is the problem?

- Students arrive at the lesson in dribs and drabs and fool around until I shout and demand quiet.

Step 2 – data collection
How often does it occur, where, when and with whom?

- It happens at the beginning of the two lessons I take them for each week. It takes around ten minutes before I can start the work for that lesson.

Step 3 – plausible hypothesis
Why do you think it is like this?

- They see little relevance in learning French.

Step 4 – action plan
What could be done?

i   I could have some games, word searches or quizzes already set out for them to start as soon as they enter the class.

ii I could give responsibilities such as handing out books, etc. to those who seem most disruptive.

iii I could send notes home whenever the class made good progress.

iv I could remind them of the class rules to arrive punctually and settle quickly.

v   I could see them all at the end of the day to make up for lost work.

Proactive techniques, i.e. to prevent it happening – i, ii and iii.

Reactive techniques, i.e. after it has happened – iv and v.

Step 5 – review

Remember: with a plan of action you are being proactive and

being proactive = control = personal confidence.

3. Accentuate the positive

Any group that is presenting a wide range of behavioural difficulties can lead adults into the negativity trap, that is that when reasoning doesn't work we shout, and when shouting doesn't work we resort to threats of detention, then if that doesn't work we threaten removal from the class. We gradually increase the punishment, believing that at some point our students will respond and do as we wish. In actual fact they are probably thriving on negative attention as well as believing that they are winning by preventing us from teaching. This is where relationships between pupils and adults are now soured. Feedback tends to be negative and everyone, teacher and pupils alike, is glad when the lesson is over. Below is a list of questions that will help you keep certain principles at the front of your mind.

1   Have you used a variety of reward systems (verbal rewards, tangible activities)?

2   Have you set clear, obtainable learning targets for the group?

3   Did you begin the lesson by highlighting progress to date?

4   Are you using a whole-class reward system?

5   Did you send any student to senior management for praise?

6   Have you sent any commendation letters or phoned home with good news?

7   Did the group help you decide the class rules?

8   Have you reminded the class of their rules?

9   Do you focus on those behaving appropriately first?

10 Are you recording signs of improvements?

4. Personal resiliency

If we look at the behaviour from a distance, a 'bird's eye view', we can discern patterns and triggers. We can look for what happened before the behaviour and what followed it. We can look for those variables that we have some influence over, for example seating arrangements and the amount of positive feedback that we give to a group. It is through increasing our understanding of behaviour that we increase our resiliency to the negative effects that challenging and disruptive behaviour can have.

Some basic facts about behaviour

1   Children are trying to solve a problem – not to be one.
2   Behaviour always has a purpose.
3   Good behaviour can be learned just as bad behaviour can.
4   Resistance to change is normal.
5   Children's behaviour often gets worse before it gets better.
6   Change is gradual – but inevitable.
7   Accentuate the positive – eliminate the negative.
8   It is the behaviour that is the problem, not the child.
9   Children with emotional, behavioural and social difficulties need advocates. If not you, who? If not now, when?

And finally some survival tips . . .

1   Stay calm and controlled.
2   Avoid letting your own behaviour make matters worse by, for example, becoming aggressive.
3   Prioritise. Work on one aspect – for example how you finish a lesson – not everything at once.
4   Develop techniques based on priorities.
5   Look at the situation from the student's point of view.
6   Assess any changes in the student's behaviour or work output – and keep assessing.
7   Use pre-prepared ways to help you think and act, for example count to ten and ask the student what it is that he or she should be doing.
8   Work as a team – talk with colleagues.

Further reading

References

Adler, A. (1957) *Understanding Human Behaviour*. New York: Fawcett.

Dreikurs, R., Grunwald, B. and Pepper, F. (1998) *Maintaining Sanity in the Classroom*. London: Accelerated Development.

Galvin, P. (1999) *Behaviour and Discipline in Schools: practical, positive and creative strategies for the classroom*. London: David Fulton Publishers.

Vygotsky, L. (1962) *Thought and Language*. Massachusetts: The M.I.T. Press.

Recommended reading

Corrie, L. (2002) *Investigating troublesome classroom behaviour: practical tools for teachers*. London: Routledge Falmer.

Forsyth, D. (1999) *Group Dynamics*. Belmont, CA: Brooks/Cole.

Index